I0032954

REAPING THE BENEFITS OF INDUSTRY 4.0 THROUGH SKILLS DEVELOPMENT IN CAMBODIA

JANUARY 2021

ADB

ASIAN DEVELOPMENT BANK

Creative Commons Attribution 3.0 IGO license (CC BY 3.0 IGO)

© 2021 Asian Development Bank
6 ADB Avenue, Mandaluyong City, 1550 Metro Manila, Philippines
Tel +63 2 8632 4444; Fax +63 2 8636 2444
www.adb.org

Some rights reserved. Published in 2021.

ISBN 978-92-9262-455-2 (print); 978-92-9262-456-9 (electronic); 978-92-9262-457-6 (ebook)
Publication Stock No. SPR200325
DOI: http://dx.doi.org/10.22617/SPR200325

The views expressed in this publication are those of the authors and do not necessarily reflect the views and policies of the Asian Development Bank (ADB) or its Board of Governors or the governments they represent.

ADB does not guarantee the accuracy of the data included in this publication and accepts no responsibility for any consequence of their use. The mention of specific companies or products of manufacturers does not imply that they are endorsed or recommended by ADB in preference to others of a similar nature that are not mentioned.

By making any designation of or reference to a particular territory or geographic area, or by using the term "country" in this document, ADB does not intend to make any judgments as to the legal or other status of any territory or area.

This work is available under the Creative Commons Attribution 3.0 IGO license (CC BY 3.0 IGO) https://creativecommons.org/licenses/by/3.0/igo/. By using the content of this publication, you agree to be bound by the terms of this license. For attribution, translations, adaptations, and permissions, please read the provisions and terms of use at https://www.adb.org/terms-use#openaccess.

This CC license does not apply to non-ADB copyright materials in this publication. If the material is attributed to another source, please contact the copyright owner or publisher of that source for permission to reproduce it. ADB cannot be held liable for any claims that arise as a result of your use of the material.

Please contact pubsmarketing@adb.org if you have questions or comments with respect to content, or if you wish to obtain copyright permission for your intended use that does not fall within these terms, or for permission to use the ADB logo.

Corrigenda to ADB publications may be found at http://www.adb.org/publications/corrigenda.

Notes:
In this publication, "$" refers to United States dollars unless otherwise stated.
ADB recognizes "China" as the People's Republic of China and "Vietnam" as Viet Nam.

Cover design by Mike Cortes.

Contents

Tables, Figures, and Boxes

Foreword

Talent and skills are valuable in powering knowledge-based economies. The Fourth Industrial Revolution (4IR) has ushered in extraordinary technological advances, fusing boundaries of physical, digital, and biological worlds to create new paradigms in the way we live, work, and interact. These trends have heralded excitement and fear—excitement in advancing frontiers of human endeavor and fear of negative repercussions on jobs and rising inequalities.

To respond to questions and concerns in developing member countries of the Asian Development Bank (ADB) on how their economies can transition effectively to 4IR, the study *"Reaping the Benefits of Industry 4.0 Through Skills Development in High-Growth Industries in Southeast Asia"* builds an evidence based on opportunities, challenges, and promising approaches in 4IR. It covers Cambodia, Indonesia, the Philippines, and Viet Nam with specific focus on two industries in each country deemed important for growth, employment, and 4IR: tourism and garments in Cambodia, food and beverage manufacturing and automotive manufacturing in Indonesia, information technology and business process outsourcing and electronics in the Philippines, and agro-processing and logistics in Viet Nam.

Much has been written about anticipated loss of millions of jobs arising from automation. At ADB, we take a tempered view. The study reaffirms a positive outlook to 4IR creating new opportunities for quality jobs. While many jobs will indeed be lost as a result of automation, new jobs will emerge through the adoption of technologies that will increase worker productivity and competitiveness of nations, thereby leading to greater prosperity. However, tapping such benefits is predicated on increasing investments in skills development and greater efforts by companies to upskill their workforce to perform new and higher order roles in complementarity with machines.

Adoption of 4IR technologies can increase efficiency and productivity. They enable real-time tracking of supply chains for production and inventory management of raw materials and finished goods. Use of artificial intelligence and machine learning can provide insights into consumer behavior to customize production. Robotic process automation can relieve tedious and repetitive labor-intensive activities, allowing time for higher order functions. Augmented reality and virtual reality can be helpful to train workers in new tasks that they were not familiar with, or skilled in, earlier. Application of 4IR technologies helps developing countries move up the value chain in their products and services. Timely skills development can ensure that automation and artificial intelligence can benefit workers at large.

The study has resulted in a suite of country reports for Cambodia, Indonesia, the Philippines, and Viet Nam, and a synthesis report that captures common elements across the four. They seek to provide policy makers with research and evidence-based solutions for skills and talent development to strengthen the countries' readiness for a transition to 4IR.

The role of governments is crucial in ensuring equitable access to skills development. We expect to see a new balance between physical and virtual workplaces as the gig economy, where employers increasingly rely on part-time freelance workers on short-term contracts, takes firmer position, and widespread digital transformation of citizen services that call for basic digital capabilities in all population groups and rising opportunities for those with advanced digital skills. Job losses will be real, however, a well-prepared 4IR strategy with industry transformation road maps that are recommended in the study can convert disruptions to opportunities to pivot the workforce to new and modern occupations.

The study was completed prior to the coronavirus disease (COVID-19). It is apparent that COVID-19 is accelerating digital transformation. Companies deploying 4IR technologies are likely to recover faster from heavy disruptions arising from the pandemic and be more resilient in the future. Beyond COVID-19, market analysts predict a 'new normal' where digital strategies adopted during the lockdown due to the pandemic will pick up pace. Consumer and producer behavior will most likely be altered permanently with greater digital exposure. The study's recommendations to strengthen widespread digital capabilities, enhance online/distance learning, digital platforms, education technology (EdTech), and simulation-based learning have become more relevant in the aftermath of COVID-19. The study also points to the scope for closer collaboration between public and private sectors, which is also quite relevant in the COVID-19 context. The findings of this study are thus very timely in the discourse to facilitate a sustainable recovery from COVID-19, as countries aspire for accelerating economic diversification and boosting competitiveness using the pandemic as an opportunity for structural reforms.

We welcome your feedback on this report and continued engagement with all stakeholders.

Woochong Um
Director General
Sustainable Development and
Climate Change Department

Ramesh Subramaniam
Director General
South East Asia Department

Preface and Acknowledgments

The ADB study *Reaping the Benefits of Industry 4.0 Through Skills Development in High-Growth Industries in Southeast Asia* marks our effort to bridge research, policy, and practice on the implications of the Fourth Industrial Revolution (4IR) on future job markets. To effectively address this forward-looking topic, the study made use of various sources of secondary information and sought to triangulate information from different primary sources. It included a survey of employers, a survey of training institutions on their readiness for 4IR, and analysis of data from online job portals from each country to assess trends in skills demand. The study used a modeling exercise to estimate job displacement and gains in the selected industries in each of the countries. A review of the policy landscape based on benchmarks from international trends and experiences provides the basis for the action points that countries can use to harness the potential of Industry 4.0 to increase productivity, facilitate skills development, and incentivize industry.

The findings and recommendations from the study point us to collaborate with our partners to implement decisive changes in renewing skills development strategies that acquire a full life cycle approach to skills development. This means that there are no degrees or certificates for life and constant renewals and upskilling are essential. The preponderant focus on institution-based training needs to give way to more flexible and multimodal training to include bootcamps, e-learning, and work-place based training. Training for digital skills at basic, intermediate, and higher levels needs a significant ramp up as workplaces undergo digital transformation.

As co-team leaders, we thank the consultant team led by Fraser Thompson, director, AlphaBeta, for an excellent partnership in this study. The core team in AlphaBeta include Konstantin Matthies, engagement manager; Genevieve Lim, engagement manager; and Richard McClellan, senior advisor. We thank AlphaBeta's national experts Ananto Kusuma Seta (Indonesia), Dao Quang Vinh (Viet Nam), Jose Roland A. Moya (Philippines), and Trevor Sworn (Cambodia). AlphaBeta's team developed the analytical model for the study and collaborated closely with ADB's team to bring new insights and directions and we are grateful for this professional collaboration.

Brajesh Panth, Ayako Inagaki, Robert Guild, and Rana Hasan provided valuable guidance to the study. We thank Shamit Chakravarti, Lynette Perez, Yumiko Yamakawa, and Sakiko Tanaka in ADB's Southeast Asia Human and Social Development Division and Paul Vandenberg and Elisabetta Gentile from the Economic Research and Regional Cooperation Department for providing inputs at various stages of the study and Sophea Mar, Sutarum Wiryono, Vinh Ngo from ADB resident missions in Cambodia, Indonesia, and Viet Nam, respectively, for their valuable support and country-level consultations. Iris Miranda, Sheela Rances, and Dorothy Geronimo from ADB, and Jannis Hoh, Shivin Kohli, and Anna Lim from AlphaBeta provided timely coordination of meetings and activities during the study. We thank April Gallega for coordinating the editing of the reports for publication and Mike Cortes for the cover designs.

The study would not have been possible if not for the leadership of senior government and industry representatives and senior members of the academia in the respective countries. We were heartened to note the high level of interest on the topic of 4IR. In each of the countries, there are already several important initiatives underway to enable industry and companies to move toward application of 4IR. The study was closely coordinated with senior government and industry participants, specifically on the selection of the two sectors for detailed study for each of the countries. The emerging findings of the study were shared in country level workshops. Senior officials and key counterparts consulted are listed at the end of each country report.

We look forward to discussions in taking forward the study's policy recommendations.

Shanti Jagannathan
Principal Education Specialist
Sustainable Development
and Climate Change Department

Sameer Khatiwada
Social Sector Specialist
South East Asia Department

Abbreviations

4IR	Industry 4.0 or Fourth Industrial Revolution
ADB	Asian Development Bank
AI	artificial intelligence
ASEAN	Association of Southeast Asian Nations
BPO	business process outsourcing
EdTech	education technology
GDP	Gross domestic product
IBPAP	IT and Business Process Association of the Philippines
ICT	information and communication technology
ILO	International Labour Organization
IT	information technology
IT-BPO	information technology and business process outsourcing
ITM	industry transformation map
MSMEs	micro, small, and medium-sized enterprises
NIS	National Institute of Statistics
OECD	Organisation for Economic Co-operation and Development
R&D	research and development
STEP	Systematic Tracking of Exchanges in Procurement
TESDA	Technical Education and Skills Development Authority (Philippines)
TVET	technical and vocational education and training
UNCTAD	United Nations Conference on Trade and Development
UNESCO	United Nations Educational, Scientific and Cultural Organization
WEF	World Economic Forum

Executive Summary

Background of the Study

The future of jobs is at the heart of the development conundrum in developing countries in the Asia and Pacific region in the coming years, and preparing the workforce of the future with the right skills and capabilities is central to the technical and vocational education and training (TVET) and skills development portfolio of the Asian Development Bank (ADB). In recent years, the influence of disruptive technologies on jobs and labor markets has intensified worries around extensive job losses arising from automation, and potential disappearance of the comparative advantage of countries based on competitive labor costs. Hence, readiness of developing countries to effectively address the transition to Industry 4.0 or the Fourth Industrial Revolution (4IR) has become an area of concern. To better understand the implications of 4IR on the future of jobs and to assess the readiness of education and training institutions to prepare for future labor markets, ADB undertook a study that seeks to capture the anticipated transformations on jobs, tasks, and skills, and to outline policy directions to prepare the workforce for future jobs.

Scope of the Study

The study covers Cambodia, Indonesia, the Philippines, and Viet Nam and includes the following features:

(i)   It focused on two industries in each country deemed important for growth, employment, and 4IR: tourism and garments in Cambodia, food and beverage (F&B) manufacturing and automotive manufacturing in Indonesia, information technology and business process outsourcing (IT-BPO) and electronics in the Philippines, and agro-processing and logistics in Viet Nam. The table shows the economic importance of each industry in each economy.

(ii) The study includes a survey of employers in the chosen industries, a modeling exercise to estimate job displacement and gains, a survey of training institutions on their readiness for 4IR, and analysis of data from online job portals from each country to assess trends in skills demand.

(iii) The policy landscape was assessed, based on benchmarks derived from international trends and experiences, for its ability to harness the potential of Industry 4.0 to increase productivity, facilitate skills development, and incentivize industry.

(iv) Recommendations suggest how to strengthen policy approaches to 4IR, especially the investments needed for skills and training, new approaches to deliver them, and strategies and actions to enhance the readiness of each country's workforce for 4IR.

The COVID-19 Effect

The study was undertaken and completed prior to the spread of the coronavirus disease (COVID-19), which has caused unprecedented disruptions to labor markets and workforce activities across the world. The study's policy recommendations and strategies to strengthen widespread digital capabilities and enhance online/distance learning, digital platforms, education technology (or edtech), and simulation-based learning have become all the more relevant in the aftermath of COVID-19. Key approaches discussed and elaborated on in the report bear great relevance to the current context of countries experiencing nationwide closures of schools and training institutes. It is also expected that post-COVID-19, there will be operating procedures in the workplace that constitute a "new normal" and will require enhanced digital capabilities. Hence, the findings of this study and the follow-on policy directions are very timely and crucial in facilitating a sustainable COVID-19 recovery strategy.

Garment manufacturing and tourism, the two sectors in Cambodia chosen for this study, have been adversely affected by the pandemic. Tourism globally came to a halt due to COVID-19. The scale of cancellations and other disruptions call out for greater use of digital tools and capabilities to help orient the tourism sector to the new normal. Meanwhile, workers in the garment industry have suffered from massive layoffs as factories are closing down due to internal supply constraints and external demand shocks caused by COVID-19. Hence, the upskilling and reskilling on 4IR-related occupations is even more urgent for the revival of the economy and economic stimulus needed post-COVID-19.

The study does not address the implications of COVID-19 in Cambodia. However, the policy directions and future investments for higher-order skills, particularly in the digital domain, are eminently suitable for the country to reimagine new beginnings for the two sectors.

Key Findings

As the study covered four countries in Southeast Asia, a report was prepared for each of country: Cambodia, Indonesia, the Philippines, and Viet Nam. A synthesis report compiling key findings and a comparative picture across these countries is also available. This report covers the key findings of the study for Cambodia. The study analyzed the implications of 4IR for jobs, tasks, and skills in garment manufacturing and tourism. These industries hold importance for domestic employment, growth, international competitiveness, and relevance to 4IR technologies. The tourism industry accounted for 12.2% of total employment in 2016 and in 2017; hotels and restaurants alone contributed 4.9% of total direct gross value added to gross domestic product (GDP). In 2018, garment manufacturing accounted for 16% of GDP and 80% of Cambodia's export earnings. The industry employed over 600,000 people, making it the country's second-biggest employer next only to tourism.

The study finds that 4IR will have a transformational effect on jobs and skills in these two industries with great potential for positive gains in employment and productivity, which can be reaped through adequate investments in skills and training. Key findings from the study include:

(i) **4IR will bring both employment loss and demand.**
   (a) Application of 4IR technologies will lead to a loss of jobs; however, it could also lead to new labor demand, and the study estimates a positive net effect in both industries. Technologies related to 4IR could potentially displace the current workforce by 12% in garment manufacturing and 3% in tourism. Automation of jobs in the garment manufacturing

industry will impact mostly manual and craft-related jobs whereas in the tourism industry, the impact will be hardest for customer-facing jobs. Both industries could suffer from negative consequences for inclusiveness as the job displacement effects are likely to particularly impact female workers. Approximately 81% of jobs in Cambodia's garment manufacturing industry are held by women. Despite the overall positive net employment effect in both industries, the study warns that there is no guarantee that displaced workers can seamlessly move into these new jobs that will be created due to automation without adequate and timely investments in skills development.

(b) The employer surveys reveal limited understanding of 4IR technologies in these two industries. For example, only 28% of garment manufacturing employers surveyed agreed or strongly agreed when asked whether they have a good understanding of 4IR technologies and their relevance to their companies. Employers in Cambodia display a much lower understanding of 4IR than those surveyed in Indonesia, the Philippines, and Viet Nam. Hence, this would imply a need to educate employers on 4IR technologies.

(ii) **Job tasks will shift from routine, physical tasks to higher-order tasks with 4IR.**

(a) The importance of routine physical tasks is expected to decline with analytical and nonroutine tasks gaining greater attention. In the garment manufacturing industry, 4IR technologies could lead to at least a 20% decline in the amount of time spent on routine physical tasks by 2030. Meanwhile, the time allocated to other tasks, such as analytical, interpersonal, and nonroutine physical tasks, could increase. This expected shift in tasks related to 4IR is not as significant in the tourism industry. Routine physical tasks are expected to decrease (as a share of a worker's weekly workload), while analytical and nonroutine tasks are expected to increase.

(b) In the garment manufacturing industry, "evaluation, judgment, and decision-making" and "critical thinking" are skills likely to increase in relative importance by 2030. On the other hand, management skills are forecast to decline in importance. One reason could be that 4IR technologies will mean that less management of workers is needed, or that more detailed data, business intelligence, and artificial intelligence or AI assistance will allow for easier management of people and resources. In the tourism industry, "written and verbal communication" is expected to become the most important skill by 2030, with declining relative importance for management skills (similar to garment manufacturing). This difference in skill importance may reflect the different ways in which 4IR may impact manufacturing versus service sectors.

(iii) **Skills shortages and skill levels in both industries need to be addressed.**

(a) While preparing the workforce for 4IR, it is important to address the overall skills shortages and the lack of preparation for the workplace. Employers surveyed in garment manufacturing (90%) and tourism (79%) reported that graduates hired in the past year have not been adequately prepared by their preemployment education and/or training.

(b) Employers in both industries stress the importance of training and skills development. On-the-job training will be crucial to deliver the required skill shift. By 2030, garments manufacturing will demand close to 13.5 million while tourism will demand 10.2 million in additional person trainings (one person training refers to training one worker in one skill from the average level required by corresponding occupation and industry in 2018 to the required level in 2030). In both industries, on-the-job training will be the critical means for skills development. Education and training institutions also need to prepare graduates better for entry-level positions.

(iv) **Training institutions in Cambodia need to prepare for the challenges of 4IR.**

    (a) There is reasonable alignment between the skills that training institutions believe will be particularly important due to 4IR and the perception of employers in the garment manufacturing and tourism industries, which is encouraging.

    (b) While there appears to be frequent engagement between training institutes and industry, the quality of workers produced appears to be lacking, which is a cause for concern. There seems to be a severe misalignment between training institutions and employers in their perception of graduates' preparedness for work, including skills required for entry-level roles as well as general and job-specific skills. While 59% of training institutions in Cambodia believe graduates are well prepared for entry-level positions, only 10% of employers in garment manufacturing and 21% of employers in tourism agreed with this perception.

    (c) In terms of training programs, 56% of training institutions reported already having dedicated programs related to 4IR skills, while 71% reported plans to develop or expand programs for 4IR by 2025. While this is an encouraging trend, it is critical to assess the quality and relevance of such training and their alignment with employer needs. A structured needs assessment for training for 4IR is needed as 62% of training institutions surveyed stated that additional financial and technical support is needed for 4IR skills development.

    (d) Quality certification of courses appears as an area of concern—65% of all training institutions believe the development of robust quality certification processes to be the most important public policy intervention.

(v) **Courses and training delivery have begun to change but further transformation is needed.**

    (a) The study found promising trends in how training institutions reported adapting to classroom teaching and learning with greater assimilation of technology, particularly digital training; 64% of institutions are using online self-learning tools. However, the deployment of advanced technologies is still limited—only 8% have adopted virtual learning platforms and only 10% are using virtual and/or augmented reality in training. The quality and standards used in these new tools are yet to be ascertained.

    (b) Training institutions have a strong focus on instructor and teacher assessment. However, the exposure of teachers and trainers to the workplace is limited. Of the training institutions, 89% conduct annual or semiannual performance reviews, but only 41% allow teachers to have time devoted to gaining practical knowledge and new teaching techniques while on the job.

(vi) **Cambodia's 4IR policies and strategies are in the right direction but need active implementation.**

    (a) While Cambodia's 4IR strategy appears to be clear in both its vision and high-level strategies, and is forward-looking and premised based on local evidence, it is less clear about detailed implementation arrangements. The degree of integration between the workers' skills and education policies is also relatively weak. There also appears to be weak coordination mechanisms between relevant government departments, as well as with industry and training institutions.

    (b) There are also specific challenges around incentives for employers to invest in the skill development of their workers, and strong emphasis on traditional qualifications attained through the education system or competency assessments, as opposed to past work experience and skills gained. There are also gaps in targeting underserved groups to equip them with the skills needed for 4IR, and in social protection mechanisms for on-demand and flexible workers.

Key Recommendations and Way Forward

Several recommendations have been identified for Cambodia to strengthen its preparedness toward 4IR to address current gaps in policy actions and enhance the effectiveness of implementation mechanisms. A multi-stakeholder approach to actions in each of these recommendations will be critical to their effectiveness. For each recommendation, a potential lead entity (from either government or private sector) was identified, along with a suggested list of stakeholders to be engaged with when developing and implementing the following recommended actions.

(i) **Develop 4IR transformation road maps for key sectors.** To better integrate the 4IR strategy with the required skill sets, Cambodia can consider the development of Industry Transformation Maps similar to Singapore, which provide information on technology impacts, career pathways, skills required for different occupations, and reskilling options for different industries. Sector-specific road maps for garment manufacturing and tourism can be a useful starting point.

(ii) **Develop a series of industry-led TVET programs targeting skills for 4IR.** To strengthen the quality and relevance of TVET programs, building on existing mechanisms for industry engagement, there can be a focus on developing courses and credentials for 4IR in garment manufacturing and tourism. These would be industry-led TVET programs specifically for 4IR, including new courses, credentials, and quality assurance mechanisms. The McKinsey-founded independent nonprofit organization Generation is a good example of an industry-led program. Over 30,000 people from 13 countries had graduated from its programs. Of this number, 81% were employed 3 months after graduation and received salaries two to six times higher than their previous earnings.

(iii) **Strengthen quality assurance mechanisms for training institutions.** A review of the 4IR readiness of quality assurance mechanisms in place in Cambodia is recommended, and to consider mechanisms to strengthen these approaches.

(iv) **Upgrade training delivery through 4IR technology in classrooms and training facilities.** In Cambodia, technology adoption in classrooms appears limited. Greater deployment of new technologies such as virtual reality, augmented reality, and virtual simulation will help strengthen workforce readiness. Given the substantial need for on-the-job training for reskilling and upskilling, it is recommended that potential digital platforms be explored for delivery of skills development. These new approaches need to permeate high schools, TVET, polytechnics, and higher education institutions. Preparation of a systematic suite of 4IR methodologies for use in training delivery would be valuable.

(v) **Develop flexible and modular skill certification programs.** It is recommended that Cambodia explore the development of flexible certification programs that recognize skills development outside of traditional education channels. A good example of a skill-based accreditation system is the Malaysian Skills Certification Program, which grants certificates to workers who do not have any formal educational qualifications, but who have obtained relevant knowledge, experience, and skills in the workplace to enhance their career prospects. Given the large-scale requirements for reskilling and upskilling, industry-led certification for gradual progression in skills is required.

(vi) **Implement an incentive scheme for firms to train employees for 4IR.** Despite the benefit of substantial productivity from 4IR technologies, employer training rates remain low due to a number of market failures relating to information asymmetries around the benefits of 4IR, a lack of well-functioning markets for training services, as well as the limited financial budgets of employers. It is thus critical to develop a set of support programs to encourage firms to invest in relevant 4IR training for their workers. Cambodia's Skills Development Fund could be an ideal platform for leading this initiative.

(vii) **Formulate new approaches and measures to strengthen inclusion and social protection in the context of 4IR.** This covers targeted interventions aimed at specific groups of individuals who may not be able to access the same skills development opportunities, and is critical to ensure that the country's journey toward 4IR does not leave anyone behind. This should cover training for three types of workers—entry level workers, workers at risk of job displacement, and workers who need upskilling—with modern delivery mechanisms, including digital platforms and industry-recognized credentials. This can build on current programs such as the New Generation Schools, the Skills Bridging Program, the Voucher Skills Training Programs, and the Basic Education Equivalency Program.

While the above recommendations apply to both garment manufacturing and tourism, there are priorities unique to each industry that should be considered when implementing the respective actions. These include:

(i) **Garment manufacturing.** Address the potentially disproportionate impact of technological disruption on females, enhance government and industry knowledge of 4IR technologies and their benefits, and support 4IR knowledge transfer from larger to smaller factories.

(ii) **Tourism**. Leverage growth of smartphone application developers to build 4IR readiness, ensure focus on training communication and social skills, and foster stronger coordination between training institutions and employers.

CHAPTER 1

The Industry 4.0 Skills Challenge

This chapter investigates the demand and supply of skills driven by to Industry 4.0 (4IR) technology adoption for garment manufacturing and tourism in Cambodia. The analysis utilized a range of data, including employer surveys and interviews, online job board data, and national labor market statistics.

In both industries, the impact of 4IR could be significant for jobs and skills. The analysis shows that despite widespread concerns of significant automation and loss of jobs associated with 4IR, the net impact on jobs for both industries to 2030 is likely to be positive, with more jobs being created than displaced. However, there are no guarantees that displaced workers can seamlessly move into these new jobs, as they will likely lack the relevant skills. Technologies related to 4IR could potentially displace the current workforce by 12% in garment manufacturing and 3% in tourism. Interestingly, the impact of automation on tourism is expected to be considerably lower for garment manufacturing, which reflects a much higher number of manual jobs that can potentially be displaced by automation. Automation of jobs in the garment manufacturing industry will impact mostly manual and craft-related jobs whereas in the tourism industry, the impact will be hardest for customer-facing jobs. Both industries could suffer from negative consequences for inclusiveness as the displacement effects are likely to particularly impact female workers. Approximately 81% of jobs in Cambodia's garment manufacturing industry are held by women.

In terms of skills, "evaluation, judgment, and decision-making" and "critical thinking" will become relatively more important by 2030 in garment manufacturing, while "communication" and "social" skills will be among the most important skills in tourism industry.

Finally, by 2030, garment manufacturing will demand close to 13.5 million while tourism will demand 10.2 million in additional person trainings. In both industries, on-the-job training will be the critical form of skills development, in particular for tourism.

Industry 4.0 and the Relevance for Cambodia

4IR is a widely used but often misunderstood term to refer to a range of new technologies impacting the workplace. The term was first conceptualized to describe data exchange technologies used in manufacturing. However, the term has now acquired a broader meaning (and sometimes referred to as the Fourth Industrial Revolution), where it refers to technologies applied across all sectors that combine the physical, digital, and biological worlds.[1]

---

[1]   K. Schwab. 2017. *The Fourth Industrial Revolution.* New York: Currency. https://books.google.com.sg/books?hl=en&lr=&id=ST_FDA AAQBAJ&oi=fnd&pg=PR7&dq=klaus+schwab+fourth+industrial+revolution&ots=DTnvbTqvTQ&sig=aOLqcUCFsLKbNpjWa 5kr2Sjzhu4#v=onepage&q=klaus%20schwab%20fourth%20industrial%20revolution&f=false.

These technologies include, among others, cyber-physical systems, the internet of Things (IOT), artificial intelligence (AI), cloud computing, and cognitive computing.

4IR is a very different concept from previous industrial revolutions, both in terms of scope and technologies (Figure 1). The First Industrial Revolution in the 18th century was marked by a transition from hand production methods to machines through the use of steam power and water power. The Second Industrial Revolution occurred in the 19th century and involved the use of extensive railroad networks and the telegraph to allow faster transfer of people and ideas, combined with factory electrification and the creation of mass production assembly line approaches. The Third Industrial Revolution occurred in the late 20th century and is often referred to as the digital revolution, involving the use of computers and the Internet, robots and automation, and electronics. 4IR builds on these past industrial revolutions but includes a far broader array of technologies that can be applied across all industries. In this regard, it is fundamentally different from previous industrial revolutions in its potential implications for economies and the workforce.

Figure 1: What is Industry 4.0?

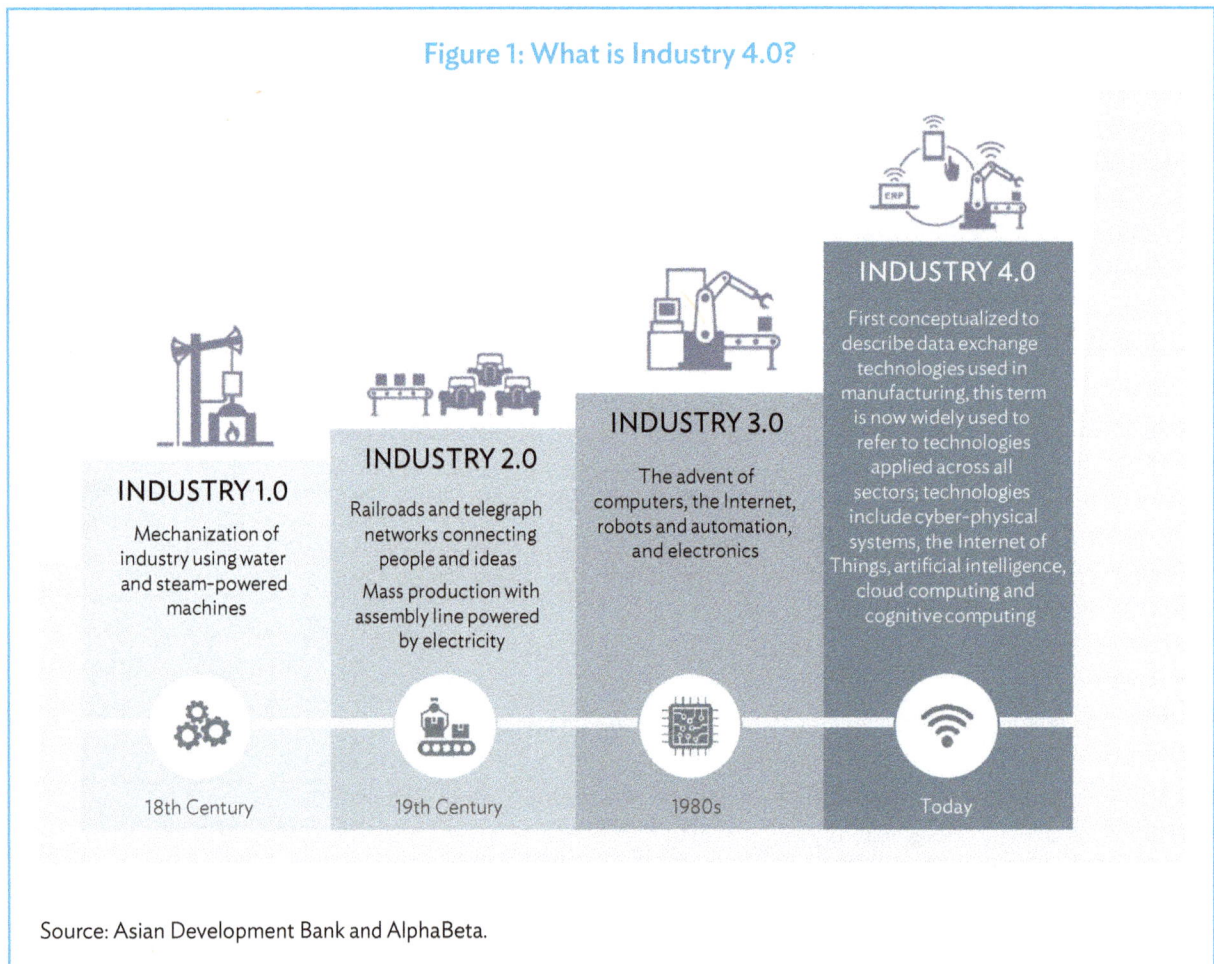

INDUSTRY 1.0
Mechanization of industry using water and steam-powered machines
18th Century

INDUSTRY 2.0
Railroads and telegraph networks connecting people and ideas
Mass production with assembly line powered by electricity
19th Century

INDUSTRY 3.0
The advent of computers, the Internet, robots and automation, and electronics
1980s

INDUSTRY 4.0
First conceptualized to describe data exchange technologies used in manufacturing, this term is now widely used to refer to technologies applied across all sectors; technologies include cyber-physical systems, the Internet of Things, artificial intelligence, cloud computing and cognitive computing
Today

Source: Asian Development Bank and AlphaBeta.

What will 4IR mean for Cambodia? According to an International Labour Organization (ILO) study in 2017, Cambodian enterprises perceived the advance of technology as the fourth-biggest economic opportunity in the period to 2025, after rising domestic demand, exports, and increased skills among local workers.[2] The same study found that 31% of Cambodian enterprises, which is higher than the average among Association of Southeast Asian Nations (ASEAN) member states, are currently actively upgrading their technology. However, only 10% of enterprises, which is below the ASEAN average of 20%, reported investing in research and development (R&D). As a result, 4IR technology adoption is relatively low across all sectors and Cambodia ranks seventh among the 10 ASEAN member states.[3] Costs seem to be the major reason as over 28% of firms cited high fixed capital costs as the main barrier to upgrading their technology. Another 20% of enterprises cited the lack of skilled technology operators as the single-largest barrier, which speaks to potential skill shortages impeding 4IR technology adoption.

4IR presents a big opportunity for Cambodia due to its current underutilization of technologies, which means there is more room for improvement. In the Global Innovation Index 2019, Cambodia ranked 98th behind other ASEAN member states including Indonesia, Malaysia, the Philippines, Thailand, and Viet Nam.[4]

With the large potential impact of 4IR technology adoption, there are concerns about the impact on employment. Most concerns revolve around fears that 4IR could lead to mass unemployment as (i) workers are replaced by machines, or (ii) workers do not have the right skills to effectively work alongside 4IR technologies or transition into new emerging jobs. According to the ILO, 57% of employment in Cambodia is at high risk of automation (footnote 2). There are also potential gender equity concerns. The probability of occupying a high-risk, automated job is approximately 1.5 times higher for women than for men.

Understanding how the skills landscape is likely to change under 4IR is becoming harder in the face of the rapid pace at which technology is developing and being adopted. This means traditional approaches of assessing skill gaps, often relying on time-intensive processes to collect data that quickly become outdated, may no longer be suitable. This study explores a new approach to understanding the labor market implications of 4IR that tries to address gaps in previous studies. Some of the key design aspects include:

(i) **Use of local data.** This study utilizes a variety of local data sources, including the Cambodia Socio-Economic Survey, the World Bank's Skills Measurement Program (STEP) survey,[5] job portal data,[6] as well as surveys of Cambodian businesses in garment manufacturing and tourism.[7]

---

[2] ACT/EMP and ILO. 2017. *ASEAN in Transformation: How Technology is Changing Jobs and Enterprises – Cambodia Country Brief.* https://www.ilo.org/actemp/publications/WCMS_579672/lang--en/index.htm.

[3] S. Chitturu. 2017. *Artificial Intelligence and Southeast Asia's Future.* McKinsey Global Institute. September. https://www.mckinsey.com/~/media/McKinsey/Featured%20Insights/Artificial%20Intelligence/AI%20and%20SE%20ASIA%20future/Artificial-intelligence-and-Southeast-Asias-future.ashx.

[4] Cornell University, INSEAD, and World Intellectual Property Organization. 2019. *Global Innovation Index 2019: Creating Healthy Lives —The Future of Medical Innovation.* https://www.wipo.int/edocs/pubdocs/en/wipo_pub_gii_2019.pdf.

[5] The STEP survey for the Lao People's Democratic Republic was used as a proxy for Cambodia.

[6] The study analyzed over 90 job profiles across garment manufacturing and tourism, scraped from the job portal Pelprek from July to August 2019, for the type and level of skills required for the job. This data was used to give an accurate picture of skill demand today and predict the trends in skill requirement changes as compared to historic data.

[7] Overall, more than 102 Cambodian businesses were surveyed. Not all respondents completed the entire survey questionnaire. The sample size used in each of the analyses therefore differed and the relevant number of observations is stated in each case.

(ii)   **Use of current market information.** Given the rapid change in the labor market, existing labor market surveys can become quickly obsolete. To address this concern, this report utilizes information on skill profiles for current occupations advertised in online job portals in Cambodia.

(iii)   **Focus on supply, not just demand.** Much of the past research has examined only changes in occupations and skills related to 4IR. This study aims to go further by examining the supply landscape, including understanding the volume and types of training required (e.g., on-the-job training, short professional courses, etc.) and conducting a survey of current training institutions in Cambodia to understand the degree to which they are currently addressing the shifts in demand for skills being seen in this analysis.

Industry Selection

Two industries were chosen to conduct this analysis of 4IR implications for the demand and supply of skills. A two-step methodology was used to select the industries:

(i)   **Shortlisting industries prioritized by the Government of Cambodia for future growth or for 4IR application.** This included reviewing the Industrial Development Policy 2015–2025, the National Strategic Development Plan 2014–2018 (Midterm Review 2016), the Rectangular Strategy (published September 2018), and the 2019 Skills for Competitiveness report published by the Asian Development Bank.

(ii)   **Scoring and ranking shortlisted industries according to a set of criteria:**
    (a) How significant is the industry's contribution to the country's employment?
    (b) Does it exhibit strong recent employment growth?
    (c) Are its exports internationally competitive?
    (d) Is 4IR of relevance to the industry?
    (e) Is the relevant data available for the industry analysis?

Industries were then tested with various stakeholders during a country consultation conducted in July 2019. Based on this process, garment manufacturing and tourism were selected for the analysis.

(i)   **Garment manufacturing.** According to the latest data from the National Institute for Statistics, the garment manufacturing industry contributed 17.8% to Cambodia's total gross domestic product (GDP). This GDP contribution has been growing by almost 8% annually since 2012. Textiles are Cambodia's major export, accounting for 67.5% of exports followed by footwear (8.2%) in 2016; the country has a strong comparative advantage in the production of garment and footwear. During country consultations, stakeholders debated whether or not Cambodia should diversify outside of garment manufacturing for future economic growth. However, there was consensus among all stakeholders that shifting from the current low-cost advantage toward higher-value added production was key, and that 4IR technologies hold much promise for facilitating this shift. It was also noted in these industry consultations that a key barrier to the successful implementation of 4IR is the current skill level of workers.

(ii)   **Tourism.** According to the ILO, the industry employed 12.2% of the country's workers in 2016 and employment has grown by 4.3% on average each year since 2014. Hotels and restaurants contributed 4.9% to GDP with an annual growth of 6.1%. There is also a strong government push for this industry to adopt and reap the benefits of digital technologies, e.g., new hospitality and tourism management technologies such as tour guide apps, online and automatic check-in systems, and inventory management software.

Garment Manufacturing Industry

The garment manufacturing industry could be transformed by 4IR. Advanced manufacturing technologies provide an opportunity for garment manufacturing in Cambodia to move up the value chain and boost productivity. However, the majority of the country's garment manufacturing businesses are unaware of this potential and even fewer businesses have started adoption of 4IR technologies.

The labor market disruption could be significant and garment manufacturing is often cited as one of the key industries that will suffer from vast job losses due to automation. This research estimates that 4IR technologies could displace 12% of today's employment in the industry, equivalent to over 150,000 workers. This is based on insights from the current tasks performed by workers and how these tasks are expected to change given the adoption of 4IR technologies (based on employer survey data). However, contrary to some perceptions that 4IR will lead to mass unemployment, the research provides an overall optimistic assessment. Net employment from 4IR may actually rise in garment manufacturing as displacement effects from 4IR are offset by employment linked to productivity gains (i.e., the income effect). In fact, by 2030, this increase in employment brought about by productivity gains could be up to 40% of today's employment. Yet, concern about inclusiveness of this impact remains as women are likely to be particularly affected by automation.

Evaluation and critical thinking skills are expected to increase significantly in demand and workers will be expected to be able to deal with problems requiring advanced numeracy. Much of this skills development will need to come from on-the-job training, but almost a third will require longer formal training from the technical and vocational education and training sector. In sum, there will need to be 13.5 million additional person trainings by 2030.[8]

Relevance of Industry 4.0

4IR represents both an opportunity and a threat to the garment manufacturing industry in many countries. On the positive side, there is a range of technologies that could increase production efficiency and develop more customized products. On the downside, 4IR technologies could see greater automation and "nearshoring" (i.e., shifting production closer to demand centers), which could threaten production in current low-cost developing country manufacturing hubs.

4IR adoption in garment manufacturing is being driven by several macroeconomic trends. These include:

(i) **Global supply chains.** Garment manufacturers have locations all over the world and Industry 4.0 technologies can enable seamless connectivity between these locations to enable operations to shift in response to production or demand fluctuations.

(ii) **Changing consumer trends.** Consumers are increasingly demanding more garment customization and faster turnaround times. Mass customization was previously cost and technically prohibitive, but 4IR technologies such as additive manufacturing can help make it less prohibitive. In 2017, Amazon filed a patent for an automated on-demand clothing factory that can process personalized orders on demand.[9] The impact of such automation technologies

---

[8] One person training refers to training one worker in one skill from the average level required by industry occupation in 2018 to the required level in 2030.

[9] CGS Blog. 2019. What Industry 4.0 Means for Apparel, Fashion, and Footwear Manufacturers. 12 February. https://www.cgsinc.com/blog/what-industry-4.0-means-apparel-fashion-and-footwear-manufacturers.

could represent a large threat to employment in this industry in traditional apparel exporting countries as production could be shifted closer to demand centers.

(iii) **Greater environmental consciousness.** Consumers are becoming increasingly concerned by the environmental impact of overproduction, and 4IR technologies can be useful in monitoring these impacts (e.g., through IOT sensors), tracing product origins (e.g., through blockchain technologies), and helping to reduce the environmental footprint of production.

(iv) **Greater competition and cost pressures.** Mass market apparel brands and retailers are competing with pure-play online start-ups, the most successful of which can replicate recent trends in clothing and provide them to customers within weeks.[10] This creates pressures to use 4IR technologies to lower costs and reduce delivery times.

(v) **Greater focus on reliability of production systems.** As facilities increasingly move toward 24-hour production, equipment reliability becomes even more critical. Industry 4.0-enabled plants will have robust monitoring systems to identify potential maintenance issues before they cause downtime.[11]

There are various 4IR technologies of relevance for the garment manufacturing industry, ranging from digital technologies enabling smart factories to additive manufacturing enabling mass customization of products. McKinsey & Company estimated that productivity could be increased anywhere from 21% to 46% through adopting industry-relevant technologies (footnote 10).

Some key technologies include:

(i) **Internet of Things.** IoT refers to the networks of sensors and actuators embedded in machines and other physical objects that connect with one another through the Internet. It has a wide range of applications, including data collection, monitoring, decision-making, and process optimization.[12] It can be used in garment manufacturing for functions ranging from supporting geo-based advertising through optimizing stock assortment, and reducing out-of-stock rates.

(ii) **Artificial intelligence and big data.** Big data refers to the ability to analyze extremely large volumes of data, extract insights, and act on them closer to real-time. This has a range of benefits in the garment manufacturing industry, including being able to use predictive analytics to fine-tune production volumes and processes, better supply chain management, and greater insights on customer segments.

(iii) **Industry robotics.** Industrial robots can significantly improve productivity in garment manufacturing. Sewing is currently the most labor-intensive step in creating a garment, accounting for more than half the total labor time. The potential for labor reduction varies by garment type, but as much as 90% of the sewing processes can potentially be automated (footnote 2).

---

[10] J. Andersson et al. 2018. *Is Apparel Manufacturing Coming Home? Nearshoring, Automation, and Sustainability–Establishing a Demand-Focused Apparel Value Chain.* McKinsey Apparel, Fashion & Luxury Group. October. https://www.mckinsey.com/~/media/mckinsey/industries/retail/our%20insights/is%20apparel%20manufacturing%20coming%20home/is-apparel-manufacturing-coming-home_vf.ashx

[11] K. Masters. 2017. *The Impact of Industry 4.0 on the Automotive Industry.* https://blog.flexis.com/the-impact-of-industry-4.0-on-the-automotive-industry.

[12] J. Woetzl et al. 2014. *Southeast Asia at the Crossroads: Three Paths to Prosperity.* McKinsey Global Institute. November. https://www.mckinsey.com/~/media/McKinsey/Featured%20Insights/Asia%20Pacific/Three%20paths%20to%20sustained%20economic%20growth%20in%20Southeast%20Asia/MGI%20SE%20Asia_Executive%20summary_November%202014.ashx.

(iv) **Additive manufacturing.** This describes the technologies that build three-dimensional or 3D objects by adding layer-upon-layer of material. Additive manufacturing allows for the creation of bespoke items with complex geometries and little wastage. Several companies are already experimenting with new apparel production systems linked to additive manufacturing. Boston-based apparel company Ministry of Supply uses thermal imaging, 3D printing, and 3D knitting technologies to create personalized blazers, shirts, dresses, and sweaters (footnote 9). Similarly, a digital image of a pair of distressed jeans can be transformed into a basic pair of jeans with laser technology in just 90 seconds (footnote 10).

Adoption and understanding of 4IR technologies across the garment manufacturing industry in Cambodia appear to be somewhat limited (Figure 2). Only 28% of employers surveyed agreed or strongly agreed when asked if they have a good understanding of 4IR technologies and their relevance for their companies. Only 6% have adopted 4IR technologies in their operations and 19% claim to have plans to adopt these technologies in the future. Aligned with ILO research, 57% agreed or strongly agreed that cost is a significant barrier to adoption (footnote 10).

The lack of understanding of 4IR is reflected by employers' expectations about productivity gains: 53% of employers in garment manufacturing are unable to estimate what productivity benefits to expect. Of those who do have expectations, these are very broadly distributed: 16% even believe that there will be no productivity improvement from 4IR over the next 5 years (Figure 3).

Figure 2: Sentiments Toward 4IR in the Garments Manufacturing Industry in Cambodia

Garment: 4IR readiness

Less than a third of employers appear to have a good understanding of 4IR and adoption is very limited, with over 50% citing cost barriers

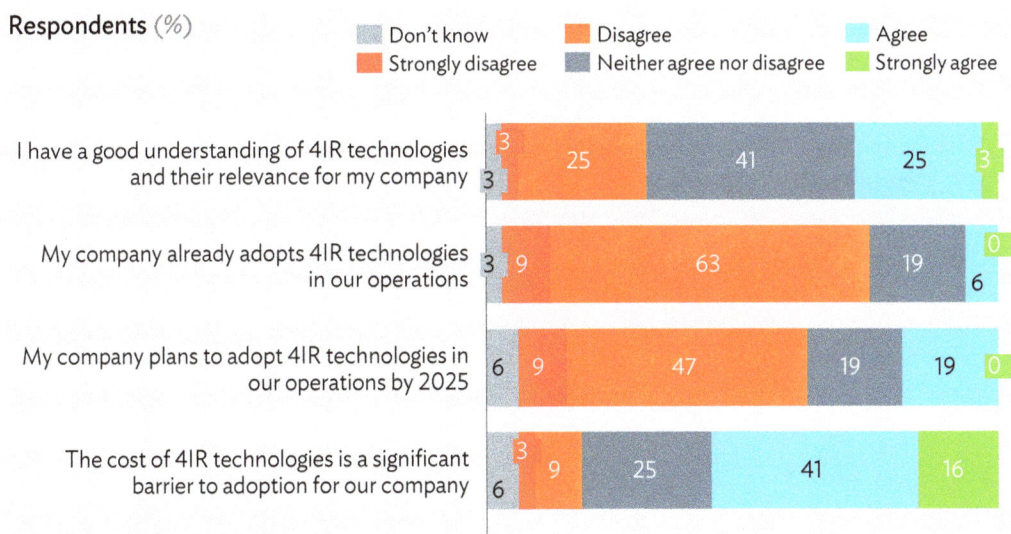

4IR = Industry 4.0 or Fourth Industrial Revolution.
Source: Employer survey on impact of 4IR on the garment manufacturing industry in Cambodia, n=32.

Figure 3: Expected Productivity Improvement Due to 4IR Technologies in 5 Years

Garment: Productivity

Over 50% of employers in garment manufacturing are uncertain about the potential productivity gains from 4IR over the next 5 years

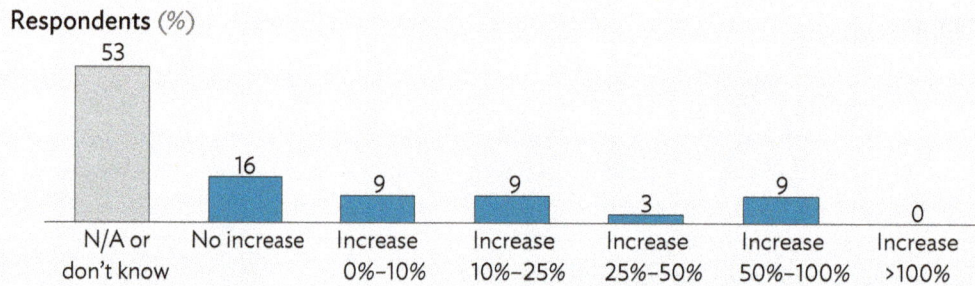

Respondents (%)

N/A or don't know	53
No increase	16
Increase 0%–10%	9
Increase 10%–25%	9
Increase 25%–50%	3
Increase 50%–100%	9
Increase >100%	0

4IR = Industry 4.0 or Fourth Industrial Revolution, N/A = not applicable.

Source: Employer survey on impact of 4IR on the garment manufacturing industry in Cambodia, n=32.

Skills Demand Analysis

Employment Implications

The analysis examines two factors influencing employment in the garment manufacturing industry related to 4IR:

(i) **Displacement effect.** This refers to the number of jobs lost due to the automation of tasks through the application 4IR technology. Job displacement occurs only if tasks automated by technology make up such a significant proportion of time spent at work, or if such tasks are so essential that a worker is no longer needed. The analysis estimates this displacement at close to 12% of today's employment, equivalent to over 150,000 workers.

(ii) **Productivity effect**. Sometimes called a scale effect, this refers to when automation improves productivity and lowers production costs. Under normal conditions, this lowers the price of goods and services, which in turn raises demand for them. To the extent that increased demand requires hiring more workers, it could offset the displacement effect from automation.[13]

Contrary to some perceptions that 4IR will lead to mass unemployment, the research provides an overall optimistic assessment. Net employment from 4IR may actually rise in garment manufacturing as displacement effects from 4IR are offset by employment linked to productivity gains, i.e., the income effect (Figure 4).

---

[13] Automation can also create new labor-intensive tasks and jobs, raising demand for labor. New job categories could emerge as 4IR technologies are introduced into production, e.g., when a more sophisticated industrial robot is introduced on a factory floor and needs programming. This is referred to the in the literature as the "reinstatement effect." This effect was not estimated in this analysis due to a lack of robust data. For further details on the reinstatement effect: Asian Development Bank. 2018. *Asian Development Outlook 2018—How Technology Affects Jobs*. https://www.adb.org/publications/asian-development-outlook-2018-how-technology-affects-jobs.

Figure 4: Modelled Impact of 4IR on Number of Jobs in Garment Manufacturing, 2018–2030

Garment: Jobs

The overall impact of 4IR on jobs is likely to be limited as negative displacement effects are potentially offset by large positive income effects

Displacement and income effects of 4IR on jobs, 2018–2030 (%)

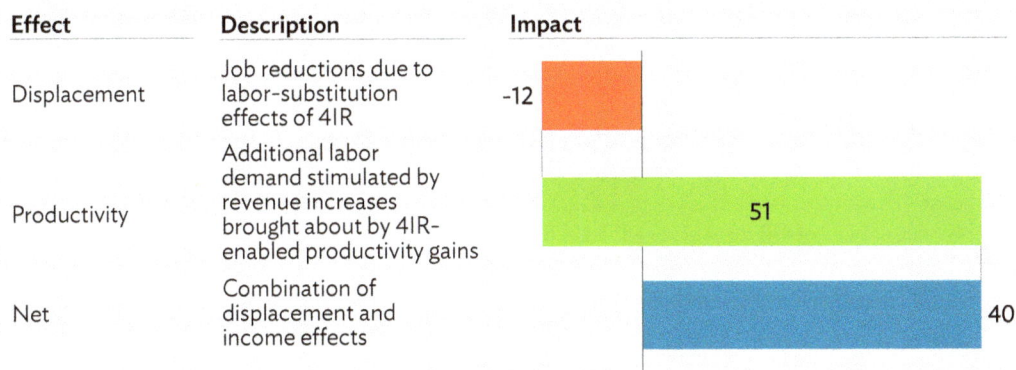

Effect	Description	Impact
Displacement	Job reductions due to labor-substitution effects of 4IR	-12
Productivity	Additional labor demand stimulated by revenue increases brought about by 4IR-enabled productivity gains	51
Net	Combination of displacement and income effects	40

4IR = Industry 4.0 or Fourth Industrial Revolution, GDP = gross domestic product, ILO = International Labour Organization, IMF = International Monetary Fund, NIS = National Institute of Statistics, STEP = Systematic Tracking of Exchanges in Procurement.

Note: Change in jobs based on accelerated adoption scenario of 4IR technologies.

Sources: Industry employment –NIS and ILO; GDP/Output –NIS and IMF Article IV; World Bank STEP survey (proxied with data from the Lao People's Democratic Republic); Employer survey on impact of 4IR on the garment manufacturing industry in Cambodia, n= 22+; Job portal data: jobs in the garment manufacturing industry scraped from the job portal Pelprek from July to August 2019.

However, even though the overall impact on employment appears to be positive, this does not mean that 4IR would not lead to large groups of workers losing their jobs. There are four critical challenges to realizing the theoretical positive income effect:

(i)   There is no guarantee that the 12% of workers displaced will be able to seamlessly move into the 51% of jobs created. The transition may not occur if workers cannot be re-skilled accordingly.

(ii)   Furthermore, the new jobs created may not materialize if there is a lack of suitable skills in the local workforce to support them. In short, Cambodia's approach to skills development will be critical in realizing a positive labor market outcome related to 4IR.

(iii)   There could be potential time lags to the implementation of 4IR, the job displacement, and the manifestation of productivity benefits. Hence, productivity gains generating additional income that make new employment possible may take up to several years to materialize, reducing the positive impact by 2030.

(iv)   Some of the productivity benefits may be absorbed by companies as higher profits if industries are not competitive, or distributed to remaining workers in higher wages if supply of labor is inelastic, meaning rather than additional employment, productivity benefits could generate higher returns for existing stakeholders in the market.

Box 1: Estimating Employment Changes

This report employs an experimental "task-based" approach to understanding the impact of Industry 4.0 (4IR) on employment. The core data sources used in this approach are the World Bank's Skills Measurement Program (STEP) survey, labor force survey (LFS) data, online job portal data, and surveys of employers in the prioritized industries in Cambodia. Unfortunately, STEP data is not readily available for Cambodia, and the STEP survey for Lao People's Democratic Republic was used as a proxy for understanding how Cambodian workers in different occupations spend their time on different tasks. The approach seeks to first understand how 4IR could impact the industry's growth trajectory, and then how employment will change based on task shifts within occupations.

The growth trajectory of the industry is computed by looking at historic industry growth as a business-as-usual scenario and then modelling the impact of 4IR as a productivity shock that generates additional productivity growth. The assumption used for the estimates presented is that adoption rates of 4IR increase to 50% until 2025, and from 2025 onward, 4IR adoption grows to 100% by 2030. This approach is not meant to forecast the actual, or even a necessarily realistic, level of 4IR technology adoption by 2030. Rather, it should be considered a thought experiment to understand the largest possible impact 4IR can have on employment and skills gaps. Productivity shocks and adoption levels were obtained from the employer survey and cross-referenced with the broader literature, where available.

Estimating the changes in employment across different occupations relies on a detailed analysis of 'task profiles' (Box 2). The analysis identifies the changes in the time spent on particular tasks from today to a future when 4IR has been adopted. Combining this with the breakdown of employment by occupation for the industry as well as the productivity growth estimates above, the result shows how different occupations may become more frequent in the industry. This part of the analysis mostly utilizes data from the STEP survey and Cambodia's LFS.

Source: World Bank. The STEP Skills Measurement Program. https://microdata.worldbank.org/index.php/catalog/step.

This impact is likely going to differ by occupation. For example, of employers surveyed, 69% agreed or strongly agreed that technical jobs in the industry would actually increase rather than be automated over the next 5 years. Surprisingly, most employers do not see the major job displacement in manual jobs, but rather in administrative jobs. Granted, given the lack of understanding of the impact of 4IR, the majority of employers anticipate no changes in the relative number of jobs of these occupations (Figure 5).

The conclusions drawn from the task shift analysis used in this report do not fully affirm the expectations of employers. In fact, the largest displacements are estimated among craft-related trade workers, considered as technical workers. In garment manufacturing, for example, this includes seamstresses. There are 173,000 craft and related trade workers at risk of being automated by 4IR technology by 2030 (Figure 6).

This could have significant consequences for gender equity. Approximately 81% of jobs in Cambodia's garment manufacturing industry are held by women, with craft and other related trade jobs having some of the highest female to male ratios. As a result, more than five times as many jobs held by females are at risk of automation than those held by males (Figure 6).

To understand what drives these results, it is important to first understand that technology does not automate jobs, but rather individual or combinations of tasks. For example, in garment manufacturing, additive manufacturing may not fully replace a seamstress but the task of preparing the first rough shape of the garment means the seamstress needs to only do the finishing touches or customization. Loss of employment only occurs if automation impacts such a high share of activities associated with a job that a worker is no longer essential.

Figure 5: Employers' Expected Impact of 4IR on Jobs by Occupation in Garment Manufacturing, 2019–2025

Garment: Jobs

On average, employers in the garment manufacturing industry expect an increase in technical jobs as well as in managerial jobs due to 4IR

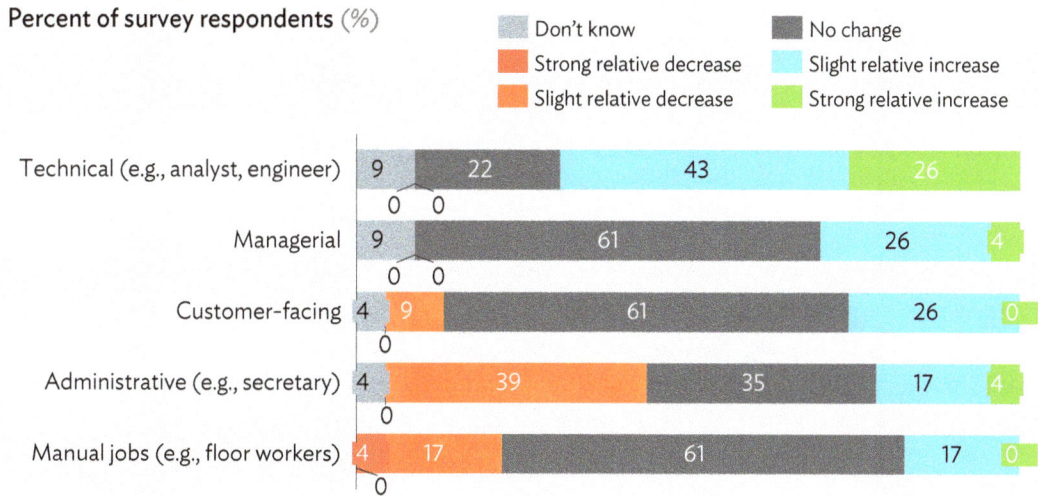

Percent of survey respondents (%)

Legend:
- Don't know
- Strong relative decrease
- Slight relative decrease
- No change
- Slight relative increase
- Strong relative increase

Occupation		
Technical (e.g., analyst, engineer)	9 / 0 / 0 / 22 / 43 / 26
Managerial	9 / 0 / 0 / 61 / 26 / 4
Customer-facing	4 / 9 / 0 / 61 / 26 / 0
Administrative (e.g., secretary)	4 / 39 / 0 / 35 / 17 / 4
Manual jobs (e.g., floor workers)	4 / 17 / 0 / 61 / 17 / 0

4IR = Industry 4.0 or Fourth Industrial Revolution.

Source: Based on a survey and structured interviews conducted with employers in the garment manufacturing industry, n=32.

Figure 6: Modelled Displacement Effects of 4IR on Jobs Predominantly Held by Males versus Females in Garment Manufacturing, 2018–2030

Garment: Jobs

The bulk of job displacement will likely occur in jobs held predominantly by women, such as craft-related jobs, e.g., seamstresses

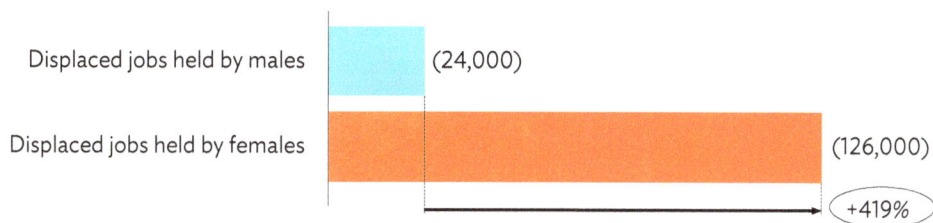

Displaced jobs held by males	(24,000)
Displaced jobs held by females	(126,000)

+419%

4IR = Industry 4.0 or Fourth Industrial Revolution, GDP = gross domestic product, ILO = International Labour Organization, IMF = International Monetary Fund, NIS = National Institute of Statistics, STEP = Systematic Tracking of Exchanges in Procurement.

Note: Change in jobs based on accelerated adoption scenario of Industry 4.0 technologies.

Sources: Industry employment –NIS, Cambodia Socio-EconomicSurvey (CSES) 2017and ILO; GDP/Output –NIS and IMF Article IV; World Bank STEP survey (proxied with data from the Lao People's Democratic Republic); Employer survey on impact of 4IR on the garment manufacturing industry in Cambodia, n= 22+; Job portal data: jobs in the garment manufacturing industry scraped from the job portal Pelprek from July to August 2019.

Job Task Implications

The research examines five types of tasks linked to jobs in garment manufacturing in Cambodia and how they could be impacted by 4IR:

(i)   **Routine physical.** These tasks involve repetitive and predictable physical work, e.g., a factory worker sewing on a manufacturing line.

(ii) **Routine interpersonal.** These tasks involve predictable interactions with other people, e.g., a call center worker reading a sales script.

(iii) **Nonroutine physical.** These tasks involve physical work that is not repetitive or predictable, e.g., a mechanic diagnosing and repairing a car engine.

(iv) **Nonroutine interpersonal.** These tasks involve complex or creative interactions with other people, e.g., supervising others, writing speeches, or creating presentations.

(v)   **Analytical.** These are tasks that vary significantly and there is a strong thinking and/or analytical component, typically involving computers or other technological equipment.

The analysis indicates a significant decrease in the time spent on routine physical tasks from above 40% to below 20% of the average work week. The decline is due to time spent on other tasks, including routine interpersonal tasks that can be automated. In fact, by 2030, workers in the industry could spend an additional 23.7% of their work week on routine interpersonal tasks as well as nonroutine and analytical tasks (Figure 7).

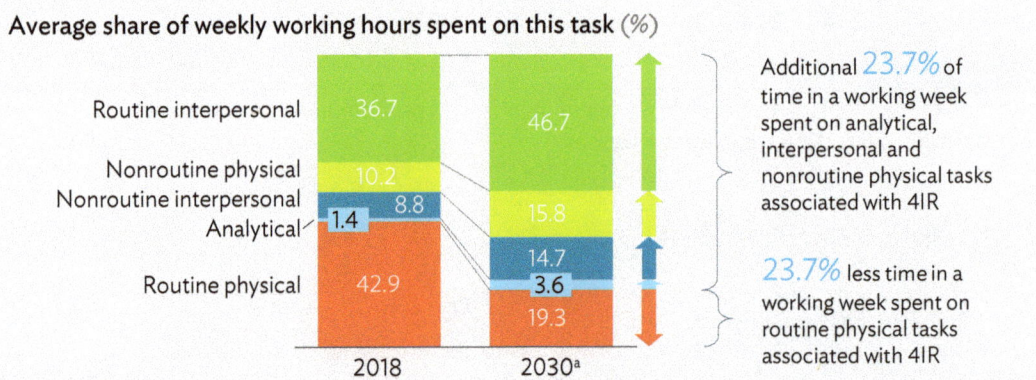

Figure 7: Shifts in Time Spent by Workers on Different Types of Tasks in Garment Manufacturing, 2018–2030

Garment: Tasks

4IR is likely to drastically reduce the time spent on routine physical tasks to shifting this time to other tasks, including routine interpersonal tasks

Average share of weekly working hours spent on this task (%)

Task	2018	2030[a]
Routine interpersonal	36.7	46.7
Nonroutine physical	10.2	15.8
Nonroutine interpersonal	8.8	14.7
Analytical	1.4	3.6
Routine physical	42.9	19.3

Additional 23.7% of time in a working week spent on analytical, interpersonal and nonroutine physical tasks associated with 4IR

23.7% less time in a working week spent on routine physical tasks associated with 4IR

4IR = Industry 4.0 or Fourth Industrial Revolution, GDP = gross domestic product, ILO = International Labour Organization, IMF = International Monetary Fund, NIS = National Institute of Statistics, STEP = Systematic Tracking of Exchanges in Procurement.

Note: Figures include rounding adjustments

[a] Based on a "high adoption" scenario of 4IR. See Appendix for details.

Sources: Industry employment –NIS, Cambodia Socio-EconomicSurvey (CSES) 2017and ILO; GDP/Output –NIS and IMF Article IV; World Bank STEP survey (proxied with data from the Lao People's Democratic Republic); Employer survey on impact of 4IR on the garment manufacturing industry in Cambodia, n= 22+; Job portal data: jobs in the garment manufacturing industry scraped from the job portal Pelprek from July to August 2019.

Box 2: Estimating Task Shifts

For this analysis, the report uses a task-based approach, which starts by identifying the employment breakdown of the industry according to occupations using labor force survey data. This provides an overview of the occupations in an industry and the relative employment for each of the 43 occupations, aggregated into five major groups: managerial; technical (e.g., analyst, engineer); administrative (e.g., secretary); customer facing; and manual (e.g., floor workers).

A task profile was developed for each occupation, which provides a detailed description of the average number of hours per week a worker spends executing specific tasks. Based on the literature, the five different task groups listed above were identified.[a] Data collected by the World Bank's Skills Measurement Program (STEP) program was used to create individual task profiles for each industry occupation.[b] Questions from the survey were used to allocate time spent on task groups. The amount of time spent on routine versus nonroutine tasks was determined, then each time allocation was further split between physical, interpersonal, and analytical tasks. The result is a profile of the relative time, in terms of hours spent, of each the five task groups for each industry occupation.

Estimates from the employer survey were used to understand how these task profiles shift with Industry 4.0 (4IR) technology adoption. Employers were asked to provide estimates of the change in aggregate time spent by task in their firms (i.e., change in the total time workers collectively spend on the set task) due to 4IR technology adoption over the next 5 years. The fundamental assumption is that the adoption of 4IR technologies changes the task profile of an occupation through automation of certain tasks and time shifted to other tasks. This results in new task profiles by occupation for 2030 where 100% of firms are assumed to have adopted 4IR.

[a] Prospera and AlphaBeta Advisors. 2019. *Capturing Indonesia's automation potential.* https://www.alphabeta.com/wp-content/uploads/2019/08/capturing-indonesias-automation-potential.pdf.
[b] Unfortunately, STEP data is not readily available for Cambodia; instead, the STEP survey for the Lao People's Democratic Republic was used as a proxy for understanding how Cambodian workers in different occupations spend their time on different tasks. Data was sourced from STEP Skills Measurement Program. https://microdata.worldbank.org/index.php/catalog/step/about.

Source: World Bank. The STEP Skills Measurement Program. https://microdata.worldbank.org/index.php/catalog/step. (accessed December 2019).

The increase in routine interpersonal tasks is partly driven by the decrease in routine physical tasks (i.e., the proportion of all other tasks increase by comparison), but also partially by the fact that workers will have to spend more time working in teams with colleagues rather than performing isolated tasks on the manufacturing line.

These insights resonate with employers' expectations: more than 50% anticipate increases in analytical and nonroutine tasks due to 4IR and 45% also anticipate an increase in routine interpersonal tasks (Figure 8).

Skills Implications
These task shifts will potentially have significant implications for the aggregate skills required in the industry. The analysis considers 10 categories of skills:[14]

---

[14] The 10 skill categories and their definitions were chosen to align with the six skill groups provided by O*NET, which is one of the key databases for examining skill changes in the workforce. Some adjustments were made to the O*NET classifications to better align with the analysis. These included disaggregating O*NET's Basic Skill group into critical thinking and active learning, written and verbal communication, numeracy, and computer literacy and digital/ICT skills, which were taken from O*NET's broader Technical Skill group due to their particular relevance to 4IR.

Figure 8: Employers' Expected Impact of 4IR on Working Time Spent on Different Tasks in Garment Manufacturing, 2018–2025

Garment: Tasks

Employers believe that 4IR driven automation will be almost exclusively focussed on routine physical tasks

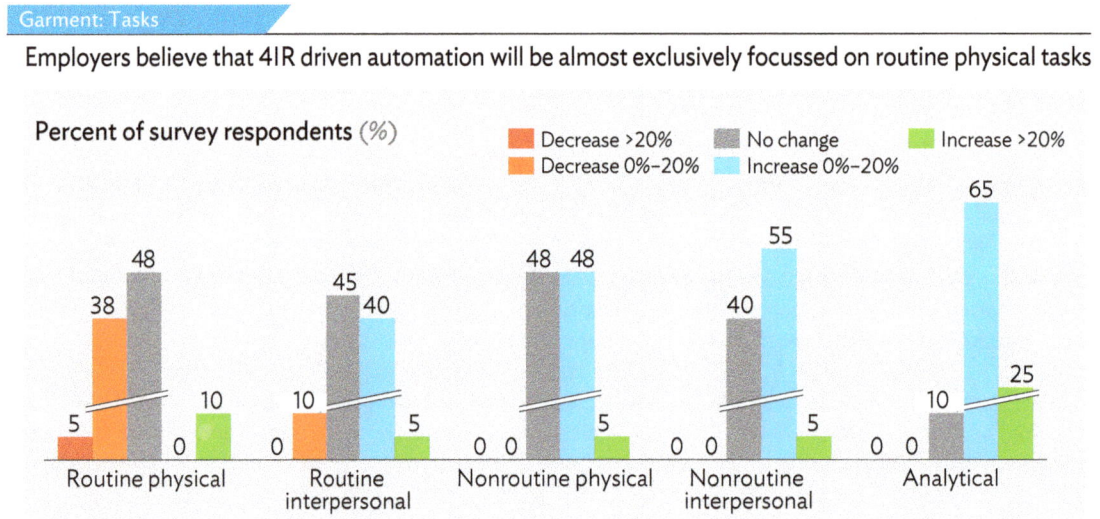

Percent of survey respondents (%)

Legend: Decrease >20% | No change | Increase >20% | Decrease 0%–20% | Increase 0%–20%

Categories: Routine physical | Routine interpersonal | Nonroutine physical | Nonroutine interpersonal | Analytical

4IR = Industry 4.0 or Fourth Industrial Revolution.

Note: Answers in above chart do not sum to 100% as figure for the response "Don't know" were not included.

Source: Employer survey on impact of 4IR on the garment manufacturing industry in Cambodia, n=22.

(i)   **Critical thinking and active learning.** Skills that allow the use of logic and reasoning to identify the strengths and weaknesses of alternative solutions, conclusions, or approaches to problems, as well as understanding the implications of new information for problem solving and decision-making.

(ii) **Written and verbal communication.** Ability to read, write, speak, and actively listen.

(iii) **Numeracy.** Ability to use mathematics, and scientific rules and methods to solve problems.

(iv) **Complex problem solving.** Skills that help identify complex problems and review related information to develop and evaluate options and implement solutions.

(v)   **Management.** Skills that help allocate financial, material, personnel, and time resources efficiently.

(vi) **Social.** Skills that help to work with people to achieve goals such as coordination, instructing, negotiation, persuasion, service orientation, and social perceptiveness/empathy.

(vii) **Evaluation, judgment, and decision-making.** Skills used to understand, monitor, conduct, and improve analysis and socio-technical systems.

(viii) **Technical.** Skills used to design, set up, operate, maintain, and correct malfunctions involving the application of machines or technological systems

(ix) **Computer literacy.** Basic computer literacy skills that allow workers to effectively use digital applications such as email, word processing, searching the internet, data entry, etc.

(x)   **Digital/information and communication technology.** These are advanced skills that allow workers to work in inherently digital occupations and perform complex tasks in a digital environment, as well as maintaining digital infrastructure such as advanced spreadsheet functions, financial software, graphic design, statistical analysis, software programming, or managing computer networks

Box 3: Estimating Skills Changes

Data from "Module 6: Work Skills" of the World Bank's Skills Measurement Program (STEP) questionnaire was used to compute for "current skill" profiles for each industry occupation. Questions from this chapter were used to assess the importance of each skill category. A value from 0 to 3 (0 means skill is not used while 3 means highly advanced skills are required) was assigned to skills based on survey responses to relevant questions. The score measures the importance as well the competency level of the skill for each category.

Future skill profiles leveraged on two sources of data: (i) data on skill and education requirements from job profiles for occupations, obtained from online job portals; and (ii) information about changes in skill requirements from the employer survey.

The collected job postings were analyzed in detail and assigned an importance/skill competency score (from 0 to 3) for each of the 10 skill categories. They were also categorized according to the five job groups identified: managerial, administrative, technical, customer facing, and manual.

In parallel, as a second estimate, survey data of employers was leveraged to understand which skill categories would gain in importance due to adoption of Industry 4.0 at an industry level. Based on the responses, percentage changes in the level of importance scores were calculated for the five job groups. Applying these to the current skill profiles based on STEP resulted in a second set of estimates for future skill profiles.

The future skill profiles used to estimate the skills gap were then computed as an average of the two estimates, and the skill gap by occupation was identified by simply examining the differences in importance scores between current and future skill profiles.

Source: World Bank. The STEP Skills Measurement Program. https://microdata.worldbank.org/index.php/catalog/step. (accessed December 2019).

Based on these skills categories above, unique current and future (i.e., post-4IR technology adoption) skill profiles for industry occupations were computed based on data from the World Bank STEP survey, job portal data, as well as inputs from the employer survey. These profiles were then compared to understand the skills gap created by 4IR technology adoption.

The analysis highlights some significant changes in the skill requirements in garment manufacturing:

(i) **Change in skills demand.** The analysis reviewed data from the employer survey and job portal to understand changes in the importance of skills linked to 4IR.
The insights from both data sources are very closely aligned with anticipated "complex problem solving, "technical and ICT,"[15] and "critical thinking and active learning" skills to see which increased the highest in importance. While employers also perceive communication skills to be increasing in importance, the job portal data does so to a much smaller degree (Figure 9).

(ii) **Overall skill importance.** Evaluation, judgment, and decision-making, and critical thinking skills are likely to see their relative importance increase by 2030 (Figure 10). However, overall there are only limited changes to the ranking of skill importance anticipated for the garment

---

[15] This represents the aggregation of the technical, computer literacy, and digital/ICT skill categories due to consistency with the available portal information.

Figure 9: Potential Impact of 4IR on Shifts in the Importance of Different Skills in Garment Manufacturing

Garment: Skills

Employer sentiment and evidence from job portal data about changes to skill importance due to 4IR adoption are broadly aligned

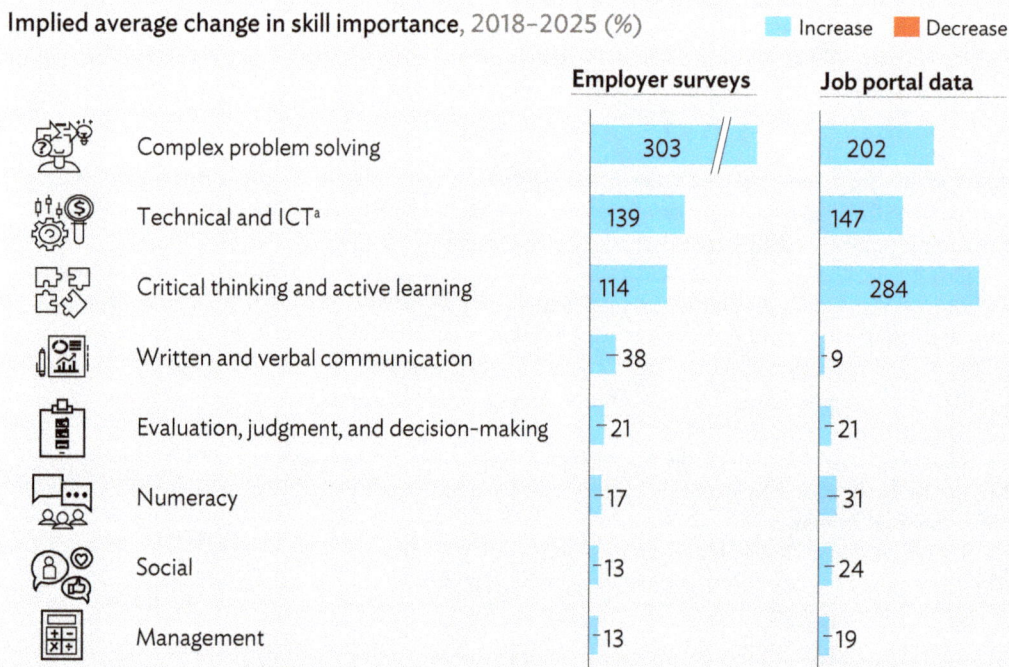

Implied average change in skill importance, 2018–2025 (%)   ▇ Increase   ▇ Decrease

	Employer surveys	Job portal data
Complex problem solving	303	202
Technical and ICT[a]	139	147
Critical thinking and active learning	114	284
Written and verbal communication	–38	9
Evaluation, judgment, and decision-making	21	21
Numeracy	17	31
Social	13	24
Management	13	19

4IR = Industry 4.0 or Fourth Industrial Revolution, GDP = gross domestic product, IMF = International Monetary Fund, ICT = information and communication technology, NIS = National Institute of Statistics, STEP = Systematic Tracking of Exchanges in Procurement.

[a] For data from employer surveys and job portals to be comparable, "Technical", "Computer literacy," and "Digital/ICT" skills needed to be aggregated.

Sources: Industry employment –NIS, Cambodia Socio-EconomicSurvey (CSES) 2017and ILO; GDP/Output –NIS and IMF Article IV; World Bank STEP survey (proxied with data from the Lao People's Democratic Republic; Employer survey on impact of 4IR on the garment manufacturing industry in Cambodia, n= 22+; Job portal data: jobs in the garment manufacturing industry scraped from the job portal Pelprek from July to August 2019.

manufacturing industry in Cambodia. Management skills are forecast to see a relative decline in skills importance. One reason could be that 4IR technologies will mean that less management is needed, or more detailed data, business intelligence, and AI assistance will allow for easier management of people and resources.

(iii) **Changes in level of skills.** Overall, the industry will require upskilling, in particular for basic and intermediate skills (Figure 11). By 2030, and under 4IR technology adoption, workers will require at least basic skills in complex problem solving, computer literacy, and digital skills. Further, communication and technical skills will need to be upgraded to intermediate level for almost the entire industry. Advanced skills are only likely to be required for numeracy (e.g., for measurements for customizations and alterations), and for evaluation, judgment, and decision-making.

Figure 10: Impact of 4IR on the Importance of Different Skills in Garment Manufacturing, 2018–2030

Garment: Skills

Evaluation and critical thinking skills will gain relative importance under 4IR while management and social skills' importance will likely decline

- Skills of increasing relative importance from 2018–2030
- Skills with decreasing relative importance from 2018–2030
- Skills with no change in relative importance

Importance ranking	2018	2030
1	Management	Evaluation, judgment, and decision-making
2	Evaluation, judgment, and decision-making	Management
3	Numeracy	Numeracy
4	Social	Critical thinking and active learning
5	Written and verbal communication	Written and verbal communication
6	Critical thinking and active learning	Social
7	Technical	Technical
8	Complex problem solving	Complex problem solving
9	Computer literacy	Computer literacy
10	Digital/ICT skills	Digital/ICT skills

4IR = Industry 4.0 or Fourth Industrial Revolution, GDP = gross domestic product, ILO = International Labour Organization, IMF = International Monetary Fund, ICT = information and communication technology, NIS = National Institute of Statistics, STEP = Systematic Tracking of Exchanges in Procurement.

Sources: Industry employment–NIS, Cambodia Socio-EconomicSurvey (CSES) 2017and ILO; GDP/Output–NIS and IMF Article IV; World Bank STEP survey (proxied with data from the Lao People's Democratic Republic); Employer survey on impact of 4IR on the garment manufacturing industry in Cambodia, n = 22+; Job portal data: jobs in the garment manufacturing industry scraped from the job portal Pelprek from July to August 2019.

Skills Supply Trends

Figure 12 shows the breakdown of the additional demand for training that will be required by workers in the garment manufacturing industry in Cambodia under 4IR technology adoption. This reflects the amount of training required to bring the industry's workforce from the skills required in 2018 to the level of skills required by 2030, driven only by 4IR technology adoption. Overall, there will need to be 13.5 million additional person trainings by 2030. The majority of the training requirements will likely come from on-the-job training, with the rest mostly coming from longer formal training, i.e., the technical and vocational education and training (TVET) sector.

In garment manufacturing, the amount of training for workers that requires only minor increase in individual skills is a significant driver of overall training needs. On-the-job-training might be the most cost-effective type of training in such situations.

Figure 11: Impact of 4IR on the Level of Skills Required in Garment Manufacturing, 2018–2030

Garment: Skills

4IR adoption will require large increases in basic and intermediate skills as well as advanced skills for numeracy and evaluation

Absolute change in percentage of workers requiring skill at level, 2018–2030

Skills	Basic (%)	Intermediate (%)	Advanced (%)	
Critical thinking and active learning	(2.0)	94.9	3.5	>50%
Written and verbal communication	(91.7)	88.2	3.4	>10%
Numeracy	(0.7)	(93.4)	94.1	≤10%; ≥-10%
Complex problem solving	92.9	5.1	0.0	< -10%
Management	0.0	(4.3)	4.3	< -50%
Social	(5.3)	1.1	4.4	
Evaluation, judgment, and decision-making	(0.3)	(94.9)	95.2	
Technical	(82.3)	90.5	0.2	
Computer literacy	93.7	(2.8)	5.5	
Digital/ICT skills	98.6	1.1	0.3	

( ) = negative, 4IR = Industry 4.0 or Fourth Industrial Revolution, GDP = gross domestic product, ILO = International Labour Organization, IMF = International Monetary Fund, ICT = information and communication technology, NIS = National Institute of Statistics, STEP = Systematic Tracking of Exchanges in Procurement.

Sources: Industry employment –NIS, Cambodia Socio-EconomicSurvey (CSES) 2017and ILO; GDP/Output –NIS and IMF Article IV; World Bank STEP survey (proxied with data from the Lao People's Democratic Republic); Employer survey on impact of 4IR on the garment manufacturing industry in Cambodia, n= 22+; Job portal data: jobs in the garment manufacturing industry scraped from the job portal Pelprek from July to August 2019.

Box 4: Comparison of Insights in the Garment Manufacturing Industry versus Past Research

According to the International Labour Organization, 88% of jobs in the garment manufacturing industry in Cambodia are at high risk of automation, compared to the displacement effect of only 12% estimated in this research.[a] One of the likely drivers of this is that rather than assuming inherent potential for automation of tasks and O*NET data, this research looks at the predictions of changes in time spent on each type of task based on employer expectations. In this regard this research is more optimistic about the impact of Industry 4.0; however, there is no guarantee that these displaced workers could seamlessly move to jobs created under the income effect.

ACT/EMP = The Bureau for Employers' Activities, ASEAN = Association of Southeast Asian Nations, ILO = International Labour Organization.

[a] ACT/EMP and ILO. ASEAN in Transformation: How Technology is Changing Jobs and Enterprises – Cambodia Country Brief. https://www.ilo.org/actemp/publications/WCMS_579672/lang--en/index.htm.

Source: International Labour Organization. https://www.ilo.org/global/lang--en/index.htm.

Figure 12: Additional Person Trainings Required to Meet Skills Demand Driven by 4IR Adoption in Garment Manufacturing by Training Channel in 2030

Garment: Training

57% of the additional demand for training driven by 4IR adoption may required "On-the-job" training followed by 29% of longer formal training

Millions of person trainings required by channel[a]

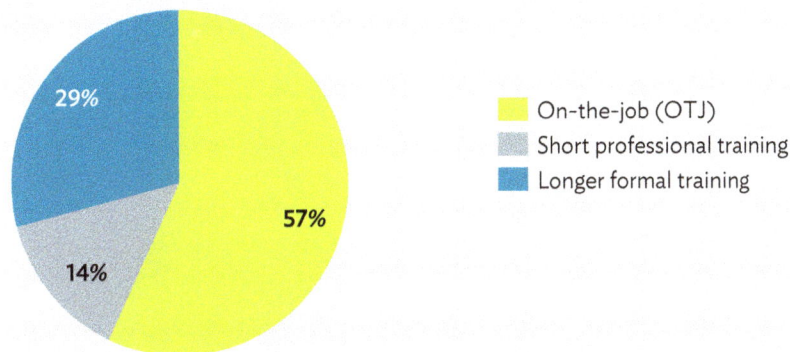

- On-the-job (OTJ)
- Short professional training
- Longer formal training

4IR = Industry 4.0 or Fourth Industrial Revolution, GDP = gross domestic product, ILO = International Labour Organization, IMF = International Monetary Fund, NIS = National Institute of Statistics, STEP = Systematic Tracking of Exchanges in Procurement.

Notes:
1. Figures include rounding adjustments.
2. One person training refers to training one worker, in one skill from the level required by his occupation's skill profile in 2018 to the relevant level given by the skills profile in 2030.

[a] "On-the-job" training refers to training conducted during day to day such as senior staff instructing junior staff or running internal seminars; "Short professional" training refers to short (between 1 day to 6 months) courses conducted by professional internal or external instructors (e.g., weekend seminars, boot-camps); "Longer formal" trainings refer to trainings longer than 6 months for which workers would likely have to take leave from their jobs, these include returning into formal education such as obtaining a degree.

Sources: Industry employment –NIS, Cambodia Socio-EconomicSurvey (CSES) 2017and ILO; GDP/Output –NIS and IMF Article IV; World Bank STEP survey (proxied with data from the Lao People's Democratic Republic); Employer survey on impact of 4IR on the garment manufacturing industry in Cambodia, n= 22+; Job portal data: jobs in the garment manufacturing industry scraped from the job portal Pelprek from July to August 2019.

Two surveys were conducted to better understand the training and education sector in Cambodia. As part of the employer survey, respondents were asked to comment on their ability to attract good candidates for employment as well as their current engagement in training efforts. Further, a separate training institute survey was commissioned (discussed in Chapter 2).

Results of the employer survey reveal a drastic shortcoming in the quality of graduates being hired into the industry, despite a sufficient volume of graduates. Only 10% agreed (and none strongly agreed) that graduates hired in the previous year had been adequately prepared by their previous education or training, and only 5% of employers find it easy to identify high-quality graduates (Figure 13). The biggest shortcoming appears to be in job-specific skills. Further, 59% also mentioned that quality of graduates can vary significantly by training institution.

Box 5: Estimating Training Requirements

Skill supply, or in other words, training requirement, can be quantified in "person trainings." One person training refers to training one worker in one skill from the skill level specified by industry occupation's current skill profile in 2018, to the required level under Industry 4.0 (4IR) technology adoption. Hence, the training required to shift a worker from current skill profile to future skill profile would require one person training per skill that needs improvement from 2018 to 2030.

To understand the type of training needed, in particular the length of training, two factors need to be considered: (i) understanding the level of skill improvement needed and (ii) understanding access to different training channels by different workers.

An individual worker's training needs are going to differ if skills improvement is required to move from basic to intermediate levels, intermediate to advanced levels, or even basic to advanced levels. For example, a worker who only requires basic technical skills at present but requires advanced technical skills in 2030 under 4IR technology adoption will likely require more training, than another worker who only has to improve his skills from intermediate to advanced level. This also applies to workers who do not need a particular skill today, but will require it in 2030, whether basic, intermediate, or advanced level.

Apart from the length of training required to obtain a certain level of skills, the access to different channels of training may not be the same for all workers in the industry. For example, workers who are displaced from their jobs may not be able to receive on-the-job training, but require formal training prior to being able to find new employment. Similarly, for future generations of workers (i.e., students currently in formal education or training), it may make more sense to embed skill training in their formal curriculum rather than wait for them to undergo on-the-job training. Three categories of workers impacted by 4IR were identified based on the skill demand analysis:

(i)   **Workers in need of reskilling.** These workers will likely lose their current jobs due to automation, meaning they will need to receive training that makes them employable in new jobs created.

(ii) **Workers in need of upskilling.** These workers will likely remain in their occupations, but the adoption of 4IR technologies means they will have to acquire new skills as well as advance existing skills to upgrade to their occupation's future skill profile.

(iii) **Future workers.** These will be additional workers that are required to fill the jobs generated from growing demand. These are workers that did not previously work in the industry, but could either join as new graduates or professional hires from other industries.

The distinction of the type of worker is an important one as different workers have access to different types of training. For example, while future workers are likely to receive some of their skill training in the formal education sector, returning to formal education is unlikely going to be an option for workers in need of upskilling, as they will continue to be employed during their training.

Source: Asian Development Bank and AlphaBeta.

Figure 13: Employer Sentiment Toward Graduates in the Past 24 Months in Garment Manufacturing

Garment: Supply

Over 40% of employers believe graduates to be inadequately prepared for entry positions and have difficulties identifying high potential candidates

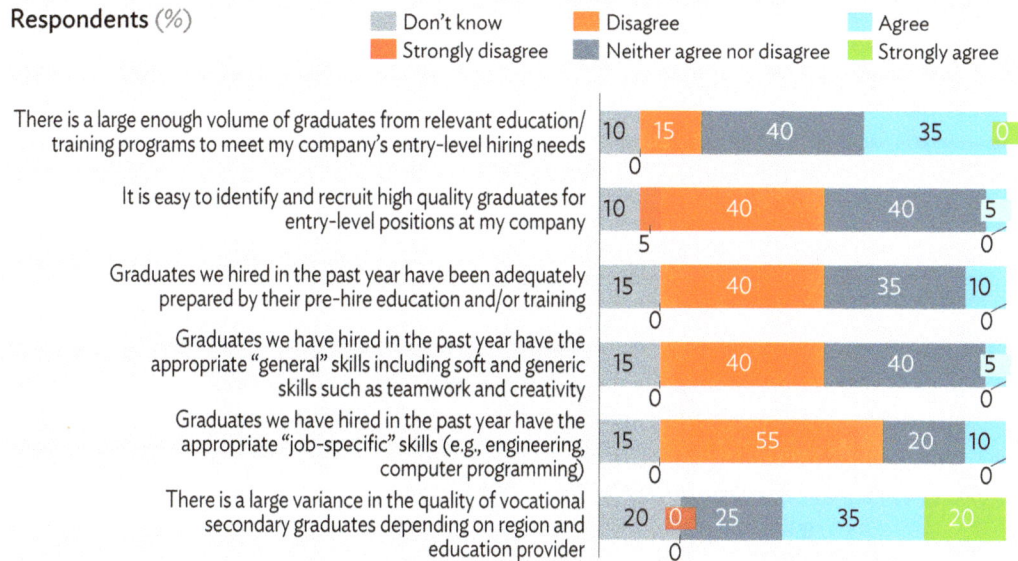

Respondents (%)

Legend: Don't know | Disagree | Agree | Strongly disagree | Neither agree nor disagree | Strongly agree

	Don't know	Strongly disagree	Disagree	Neither agree nor disagree	Agree	Strongly agree
There is a large enough volume of graduates from relevant education/training programs to meet my company's entry-level hiring needs	10	0	15	40	35	0
It is easy to identify and recruit high quality graduates for entry-level positions at my company	10	5	40	40	5	0
Graduates we hired in the past year have been adequately prepared by their pre-hire education and/or training	15	0	40	35	10	0
Graduates we have hired in the past year have the appropriate "general" skills including soft and generic skills such as teamwork and creativity	15	0	40	40	5	0
Graduates we have hired in the past year have the appropriate "job-specific" skills (e.g., engineering, computer programming)	15	0	55	20	10	0
There is a large variance in the quality of vocational secondary graduates depending on region and education provider	20	0	0	25	35	20

Source: Employer survey on impact of Industry 4.0 on the garment manufacturing industry in Cambodia, n=20.

Tourism Industry

Results from the tourism industry differ from the garment manufacturing industry in some significant ways. Similar to garment manufacturing, employers in the tourism industry in Cambodia also show low levels of current understanding of 4IR technologies and adoption.

However, while the overall impact on employment is estimated to also be net positive (similar to garment manufacturing), the displacement and income effect in tourism are much smaller, meaning the industry is likely to experience much less disruption due to 4IR. These smaller changes are partially driven by less drastic task shifts than what was observed in garment manufacturing. Being a service industry, the impact of automation in tourism is likely to be felt mainly on customer-facing jobs, which tend to be held mostly by women, thus creating adverse effects on inclusiveness in the industry.

Compared to garment manufacturing, communication and social skills are likely to be of far greater importance in tourism under 4IR technology adoption, requiring far more workers with advanced skills. Due to limited job displacement and new workers joining the industry as a result of 4IR, much of the additional training required will have to take place on the job, meaning the TVET sector may have to consider adjusting its offering to these workers. A significant amount of additional training from 2018 to 2030 will be required. Overall, there will need to be 10.2 million additional person trainings by 2030.

Relevance to Industry 4.0

While 4IR has largely been focused on manufacturing industries, it can also have dramatic effects on the service sector. The tourism industry is a good example; in a way, tourism is already at the forefront of digital change. For example, 82% of travel bookings in 2018 were completed online or via mobile, without human interaction.[16] 4IR technologies could potentially broaden the impact beyond just online or mobile applications to transform the entire tourism value chain. This is also driven by technologies that, for example, provide a more seamless customer experience in booking trips (particularly in remote locations) or allow service providers to hire qualified staff.

There are various 4IR technologies of relevance for the tourism industry, ranging from big data analysis and simulations that can enhance service delivery, to mobile internet technologies that can transform the ways in which consumers get access to and purchase tourism services.

Some key technologies include:

(i) **Facial recognition and biometric data.** Facial recognition technology is a form of biometric artificial intelligence, which is able to identify an individual or verify their identity based on facial features. This technology can be used to increase personalization of services (e.g., a concierge is able to greet the guest by name on arrival), security (e.g., 77% of airports and 71% of airlines are planning major programs, or research or development around biometric ID management over the next 5 years),[17] data analysis, and payments. MasterCard has already began experimenting with a "selfie pay" system, where payments can be confirmed using a smartphone camera, with the image being matched to a database.[18]

(ii) **Blockchain technology.** Blockchain technology refers to a list of public records, also known as a public ledger, wherein transactions between parties are listed or stored. Each record, or referred to as "block," is secured using cryptography. Blockchain can make accessing and storing important information easier and more reliable (e.g., payment information, passport details, baggage information) because responsibility for storing it is shared across the whole network.[19]

(iii) **Internet of Things.** The Internet of Things (IoT) refers to networks of sensors and actuators embedded in machines and other physical objects that connect with one another via the Internet. It can be used in tourism to provide personalization of services, seamless travel (e.g., real-time information on baggage), energy savings in hotels, location-specific marketing, and real-time maintenance and repairs.[20]

(iv) **Big data.** Big data refers to the ability to analyze extremely large volumes of data, extract insights, and act on them closer to real-time. This provides a range of benefits in the tourism industry, including being able to use predictive analytics on occupancy and greater insights on customer segments. The Dorchester Collection hotel, for instance, has used artificial intelligence (AI) technologies and big data to sort through customer feedback from surveys, reviews, and online polls, to build a clearer picture of current customer opinion in real-time.[21]

---

[16]   TrekkSoft. 2019. *Travel Trends Report 2019*. https://www.trekksoft.com/en/resources/ebooks/travel-trends-report-2019.

[17]   SITA. 2018. *Air Transport IT Insights 2018*. https://www.sita.aero/resources/type/surveys-reports/air-transport-it-insights-2018.

[18]   Revfine. 2018. *4 Ways Facial Recognition Can Be Used in the Travel Industry*. https://www.revfine.com/facial-recognition-travel-industry/.

[19]   Revfine. 2018. *How Blockchain Technology is Transforming the Travel Industry*. https://www.revfine.com/blockchain-technology-travel-industry/.

[20]   Revfine. 2018. *How the Internet of Things (IoT) can Benefit the Travel Industry*. https://www.revfine.com/internet-of-things-travel-industry/.

[21]   Revfine. 2018. *How Artificial Intelligence is Changing the Travel Industry*. https://www.revfine.com/artificial-intelligence-travel-industry/.

(v) **Internet and mobile technology.** Finding travel accommodations can be a protracted and challenging process for most consumers—McKinsey estimates that an average purchase journey for a single hotel room lasts 36 days with 45 touch points, distributed among search engines and the websites of intermediaries and suppliers, and involves multiple devices.[22] AI technologies fused with internet and mobile technologies could significantly improve the efficiency of the search experience. There has already been widespread adoption of AI technologies for the purposes of powering "chatbots" on social media platforms as well as instant messaging apps. This can help companies respond to consumer demands for faster response times and enable 24/7 access.

(vi) **Industry robotics.** While industrial robots are currently focused on heavy manufacturing industries, as the technology evolves and robots become more adaptable, there could be greater investment in robots in service industries like tourism. In tourism, it is highly probable that robots will be able to carry out strenuous and unattractive jobs such as waiting on tables, cleaning, and garbage disposal.[23] Hilton Hotels, for example, has deployed an interactive AI robot named Connie, which uses AI and speech recognition to provide customers with tourist information. The robot absorbs data through human interaction, helping to improve the quality of communications (footnote 21).

(vii) **Virtual reality.** Virtual reality involves the full immersion in computerized programs that provide contact in real-time. This could be used by tourism operators to share experiences and better market to end-consumers.

Understanding of the relevance of 4IR to the tourism industry appears to also be mixed among employers. While 43% of employers agreed with the statement that their companies have already adopted 4IR technologies, only 35% said they have a good understanding of these technologies (Figure 14). On closer inspection of survey responses, it appears that many employers are uncertain about the distinction between 4IR and general digitalization under Industry 3.0 (e.g., using computers, internet access, etc.), which can potentially explain discrepancies in the data. Only 19% of employers surveyed are planning to adopt 4IR over the next 5 years.

In line with the general uncertainty about 4IR, 43% of employers are also uncertain about potential productivity gains (Figure 15). Even those that do have expectations estimate potential productivity gains for Cambodia over the next 5 years to be small. Close to 50% expect the productivity gains to be less than 50%.

Skills Demand Analysis

Employment Implications
The impact of 4IR technology on employment in the tourism industry in Cambodia is likely to be net positive, although different and significantly smaller than other industries (Figure 16). Only around 3% of jobs are at risk of displacement from automation. The overall effect on employment is likely to be net positive, expected to increase by around 2% of current jobs predicted by 2030 due to 4IR. However, given the same challenges on positive productivity effect as in the garment manufacturing industry, skilling approaches will play an important role in tourism.

22 A. Dichter. 2018. How to Serve Today's Digital Traveler. *McKinsey & Company.* 19 December. https://www.mckinsey.com/industries/travel-transport-and-logistics/our-insights/how-to-serve-todays-digital-traveler.
23 Gül and Gül. 2018. The effect of the Fourth Industrial Revolution on Tourism. *Balikesir University Working Paper Series.* http://nbuv.gov.ua/j-pdf/evdvnz_2018_2_8.pdf.

Figure 14: Sentiments Toward 4IR in the Tourism Industry

Tourism: 4IR readiness

Only 35% of employers in the tourism industry believe to have a good understanding of 4IR but 43% have already adopted some technologies

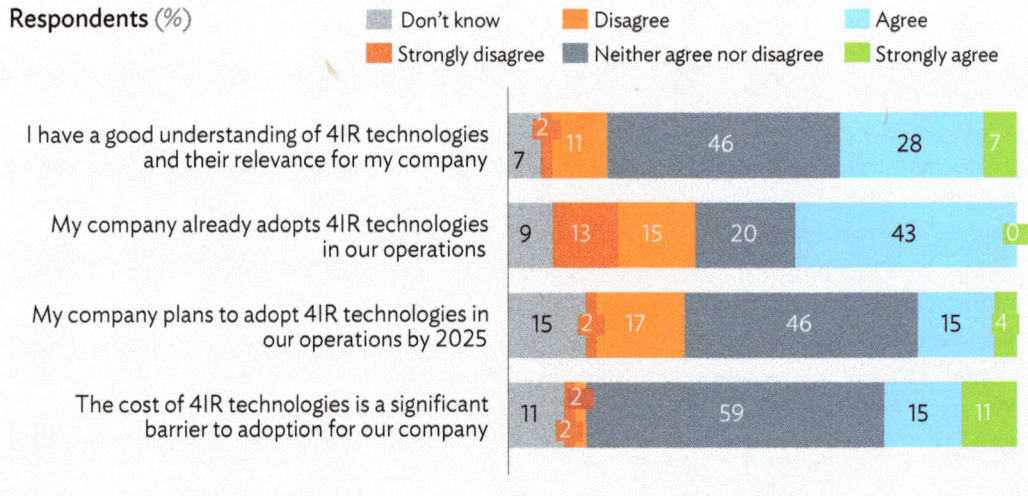

Respondents (%)

Legend: Don't know | Disagree | Agree | Strongly disagree | Neither agree nor disagree | Strongly agree

Statement	Strongly disagree	Disagree	Neither	Agree	Strongly agree	Don't know
I have a good understanding of 4IR technologies and their relevance for my company	7	2, 11	46	28	7	
My company already adopts 4IR technologies in our operations	9	13, 15	20	43	0	
My company plans to adopt 4IR technologies in our operations by 2025	15	2, 17	46	15	4	
The cost of 4IR technologies is a significant barrier to adoption for our company	11	2, 2	59	15	11	

4IR = Industry 4.0 or Fourth Industrial Revolution.

Source: Employer survey on impact of 4IR on the tourism industry in Cambodia, n=46.

Figure 15: Expected Productivity Improvement Due to 4IR in 5 Years

Tourism: Jobs

43% of employers in the tourism industry are uncertain about the productivity impact of 4IR and 50% believe the impact to be less than 50%

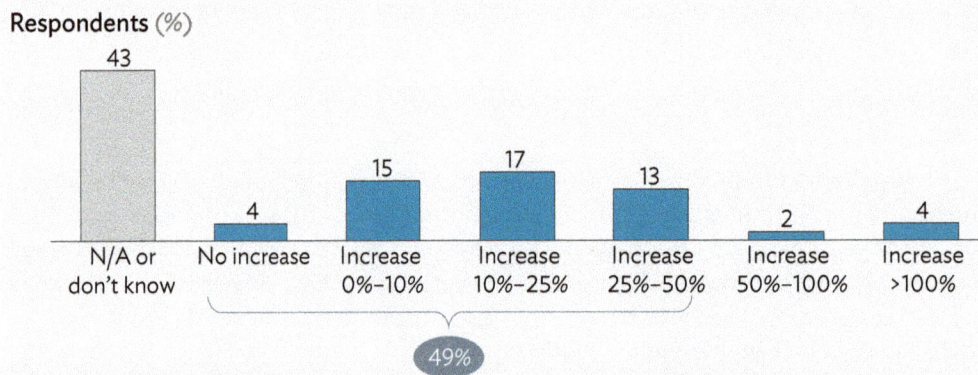

Respondents (%)

N/A or don't know	No increase	Increase 0%–10%	Increase 10%–25%	Increase 25%–50%	Increase 50%–100%	Increase >100%
43	4	15	17	13	2	4

49%

4IR = Industry 4.0 or Fourth Industrial Revolution, N/A = not applicable.

Source: Employer survey on impact of 4IR on the tourism industry in Cambodia, n=46.

Figure 16: Modelled Impact of 4IR on Number of Jobs in Tourism, 2018–2030

Tourism: Jobs

The overall impact of 4IR on jobs is likely to be small and marginally positive as displacement is potentially offset by income effects

Displacement and income effects of 4IR on jobs, 2018–2030 (%)

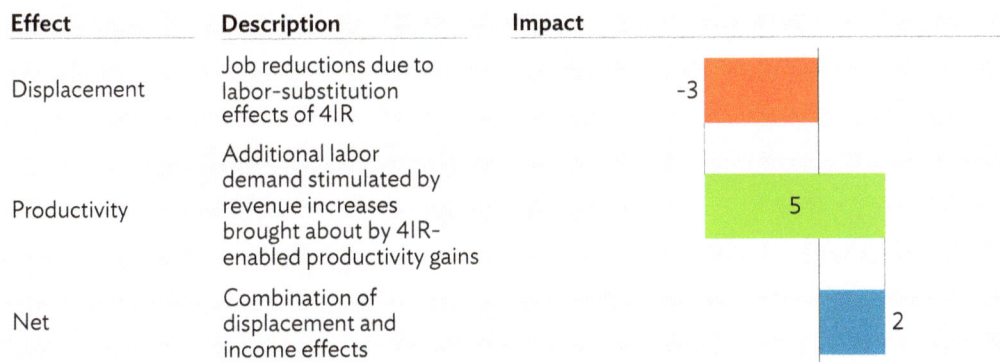

Effect	Description	Impact
Displacement	Job reductions due to labor-substitution effects of 4IR	-3
Productivity	Additional labor demand stimulated by revenue increases brought about by 4IR-enabled productivity gains	5
Net	Combination of displacement and income effects	2

4IR = Industry 4.0 or Fourth Industrial Revolution, GDP = gross domestic product, ILO = International Labour Organization, IMF = International Monetary Fund, NIS = National Institute of Statistics, STEP = Systematic Tracking of Exchanges in Procurement.

Note: Change in jobs based on accelerated adoption scenario of 4IR technologies.

Sources: Industry employment –NIS, Cambodia Socio-EconomicSurvey (CSES) 2017and ILO; GDP/Output –NIS, McKinsey and IMF Article IV; World Bank STEP survey (proxied with data from the Lao People's Democratic Republic); Employer survey on impact of 4IR on the tourism industry in Cambodia, n= 39+; Job portal data: jobs in the tourism industry scraped from the job portal Pelprek from July to August 2019.

While 4IR technologies are relevant for the tourism industry, implementation could be more challenging in the services sector (compared to the manufacturing sector) due to the variety of roles and lack of standardized procedures. In addition, workers currently spread their time across a range of different tasks, so 4IR technologies impacting one type of tasks (e.g., routine physical tasks) is unlikely to lead to a loss of employment, but a shift of focus to other tasks.

Given the same challenges on positive productivity effect as in the garment manufacturing industry, Cambodia's approach to skill development will be critical in realizing a positive labor-market outcome related to 4IR in tourism. Only with suitable skills will displaced workers be able to seamlessly move into newly created jobs.

However, despite the total size of displacement being far less disruptive than in other sectors, there is a real concern about implications on inclusiveness (Figure 17). Given the service-centric nature of the industry, it is not surprising that customer-facing occupations are most impacted by 4IR technology adoption. In Cambodia, these occupations are mostly held by women, meaning the displacement impact on women could be twice as large as that for men.

Figure 17: Modelled Displacement Effects of 4IR on Jobs Predominantly Held by Males versus Females in Tourism, 2018–2030

Tourism: Jobs

Based on the analysis, twice as many jobs will be replaced in occupations that are more likely held by women

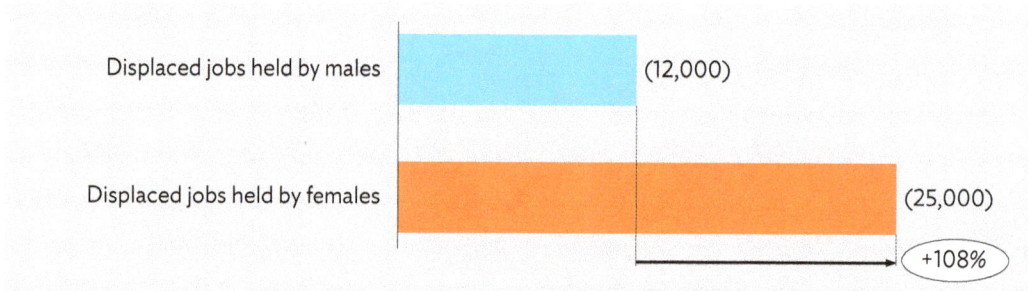

Displaced jobs held by males   (12,000)

Displaced jobs held by females   (25,000)   +108%

4IR = Industry 4.0 or Fourth Industrial Revolution, GDP = gross domestic product, ILO = International Labour Organization, IMF = International Monetary Fund, NIS = National Institute of Statistics, STEP = Systematic Tracking of Exchanges in Procurement.

Note: Change in jobs based on accelerated adoption scenario of Industry 4.0 technologies.

Sources: Industry employment –NIS, Cambodia Socio-EconomicSurvey (CSES) 2017and ILO; GDP/Output –NIS, McKinsey and IMF Article IV; World Bank STEP survey (proxied with data from the Lao People's Democratic Republic); Employer survey on impact of 4IR on the tourism industry in Cambodia, n= 39+; Job portal data: jobs in the tourism industry scraped from the job portal Pelprek from July to August 2019.

Job Task Implications

The task shifts estimated for the tourism industry are far less drastic than for the garment manufacturing industry (Figure 18). On aggregate, analytical and nonroutine tasks will increase, while routine interpersonal tasks will decrease. According to the results, workers in the industry could spend an additional 6.5% of their work week on analytical nonroutine tasks versus routine tasks.

This is consistent with insights from the employer survey, with employers expecting 24% routine physical tasks and 43% of routine interpersonal tasks to decline in the future due to 4IR (Figure 19). Again there appears to be a high degree of uncertainty about the impact of 4IR in particular on physical tasks as 73% of employers predict no change on routine tasks and 57% predict likewise predict no changes to nonroutine physical tasks.

Skills Implications

The analysis highlights some significant changes in skill requirements in the tourism industry:

(i)   **Change in skills demand.** According to employers, technical and ICT,[24] complex problem solving, and critical thinking skills will see the highest increases in importance over the next 5 years. This resonates with data extracted from online job portals. However, results are more varied for the remaining categories of skills. Online job portal data predict decreases in the

---

[24]   This represents the aggregation of the technical, computer literacy, and digital/ICT skill categories due to consistency with the available portal information.

Figure 18: Shifts in Time Spent by Workers on Different Types of Tasks in Tourism, 2018–2030

Tourism: Tasks

4IR application in the tourism industry will likely lead to shifts from time spent on routine to nonroutine and analytical tasks

Average share of weekly working hours spent on this task (%)

Task	2018	2030ᵃ
Analytical	13.8	16.7
Nonroutine interpersonal	12.9	16.0
Nonroutine physical	8.3	8.8
Routine physical	24.6	22.5
Routine interpersonal	40.4	36.0

Additional 6.5% of time in a working week spent on analytical and nonroutine tasks associated with 4IR

6.5% less time in a working week spent on routine tasks associated with 4IR

4IR = Industry 4.0 or Fourth Industrial Revolution, GDP = gross domestic product, ILO = International Labour Organization, IMF = International Monetary Fund, NIS = National Institute of Statistics, STEP = Systematic Tracking of Exchanges in Procurement.

Note: Figures include rounding adjustments.

ᵃ Based on a "high adoption" scenario of 4IR. See Appendix for details.

Sources: Industry employment –NIS, Cambodia Socio-EconomicSurvey (CSES) 2017and ILO; GDP/Output –NIS, McKinsey and IMF Article IV; World Bank STEP survey (proxied with data from the Lao People's Democratic Republic); Employer survey on impact of 4IR on the tourism industry in Cambodia, n= 39+; Job portal data: jobs in the tourism industry scraped from the job portal Pelprek from July to August 2019.

Figure 19: Employers' Expected Impact of 4IR on Working Time Spent on Different Tasks in Tourism, 2018–2030

Tourism: Tasks

With the exception of nonroutine interpersonal and analytical tasks increasing, there is a lot of uncertainty about skills shifts from 4IR

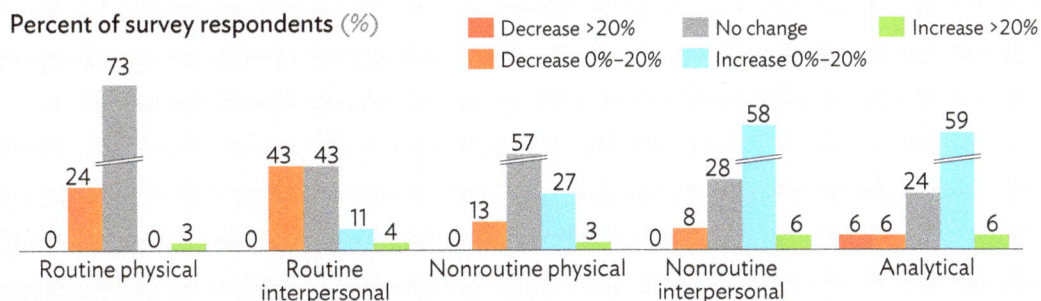

Percent of survey respondents (%)

Legend: Decrease >20% | No change | Increase >20% | Decrease 0%–20% | Increase 0%–20%

	Routine physical	Routine interpersonal	Nonroutine physical	Nonroutine interpersonal	Analytical
Decrease >20%	0	0	0	0	6
Decrease 0%–20%	24	43	13	8	6
No change	73	43	57	28	24
Increase 0%–20%	0	11	27	58	59
Increase >20%	3	4	3	6	6

4IR = Industry 4.0 or Fourth Industrial Revolution.

Note: Answers in this figure do not sum to 100% as numbers for the response "Don't know" were not included.

Source: Employer survey on impact of 4IR on the tourism industry in Cambodia, n=39.

Figure 20: Potential Impact of 4IR on Shifts in the Importance of Different Skills in Tourism

Tourism: Skills

Employers and job portal data seem aligned on future skills of importance,
however, job portals indicate declines in management and evaluation skills

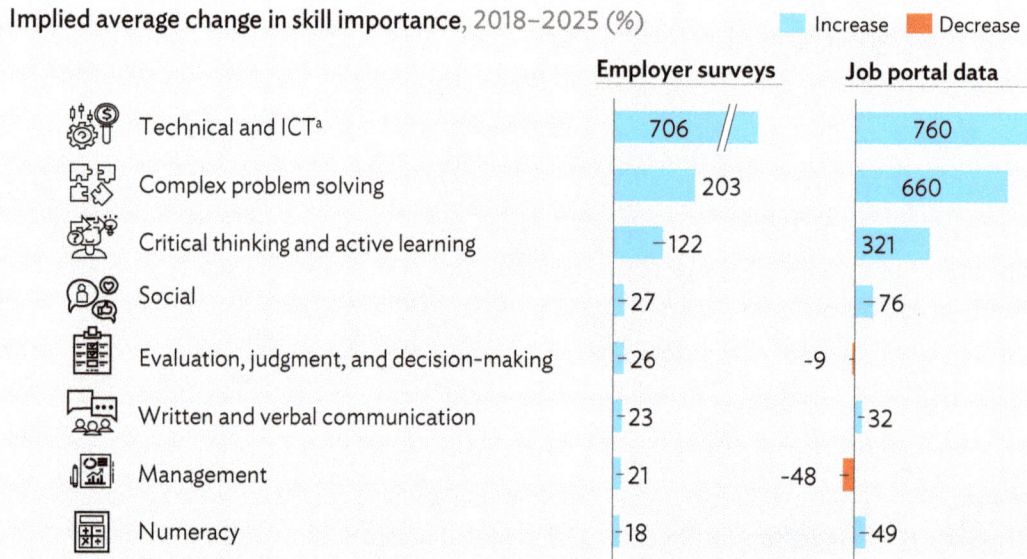

Implied average change in skill importance, 2018–2025 (%)   ■ Increase ■ Decrease

	Employer surveys	Job portal data
Technical and ICT[a]	706	760
Complex problem solving	203	660
Critical thinking and active learning	122	321
Social	27	76
Evaluation, judgment, and decision-making	26	−9
Written and verbal communication	23	32
Management	21	−48
Numeracy	18	49

4IR = Industry 4.0 or Fourth Industrial Revolution, GDP = gross domestic product, ILO = International Labour Organization, IMF = International Monetary Fund, ICT = information and communication technology, NIS = National Institute of Statistics, STEP = Systematic Tracking of Exchanges in Procurement.

[a] For data from employer surveys and job portals to be comparable, "Technical", "Computer literacy," and "Digital/ICT" skills needed to be aggregated.

Sources: Industry employment –NIS, Cambodia Socio-EconomicSurvey (CSES) 2017and ILO; GDP/Output –NIS, McKinsey and IMF Article IV; World Bank STEP survey (proxied with data from the Lao People's Democratic Republic); Employer survey on impact of 4IR on the tourism industry in Cambodia, n= 39+; Job portal data: jobs in the tourism industry scraped from the job portal Pelprek from July to August 2019.

importance of management, and evaluation, judgment, and decision-making skills (Figure 20). As expected, social skills are expected to increase higher in importance for tourism than for garment manufacturing.

(ii) **Overall skill importance.** Communication and social skills will increase in their relative ranking under 4IR technology adoption. Communication is expected to become the most important skill in 2030, with management skills declining in relative importance significantly (Figure 21). Interestingly and somewhat at odds with employers' expectations, computer literacy and complex problem solving are estimated to decline in ranking according to relative importance, surpassed by critical thinking and technical skills. These changes are very much aligned with the task shifts observed above.

(iii) **Changes in level of skills.** Overall, the industry will require significant upskilling as the demand for more intermediate and advanced skills is likely to increase (Figure 22). The main skills requiring advanced levels by 2030 under 4IR will be communication, social, and evaluation skills. More than half of workers in the industry will be expected to have intermediate technical and ICT as well as critical thinking skills.

Figure 21: Impact of 4IR on the Importance of Different Skills in Tourism, 2018–2030

Tourism: Skills

Communication and social skills are likely to be of greater relative importance under 4IR as workers have tofocus on customer service

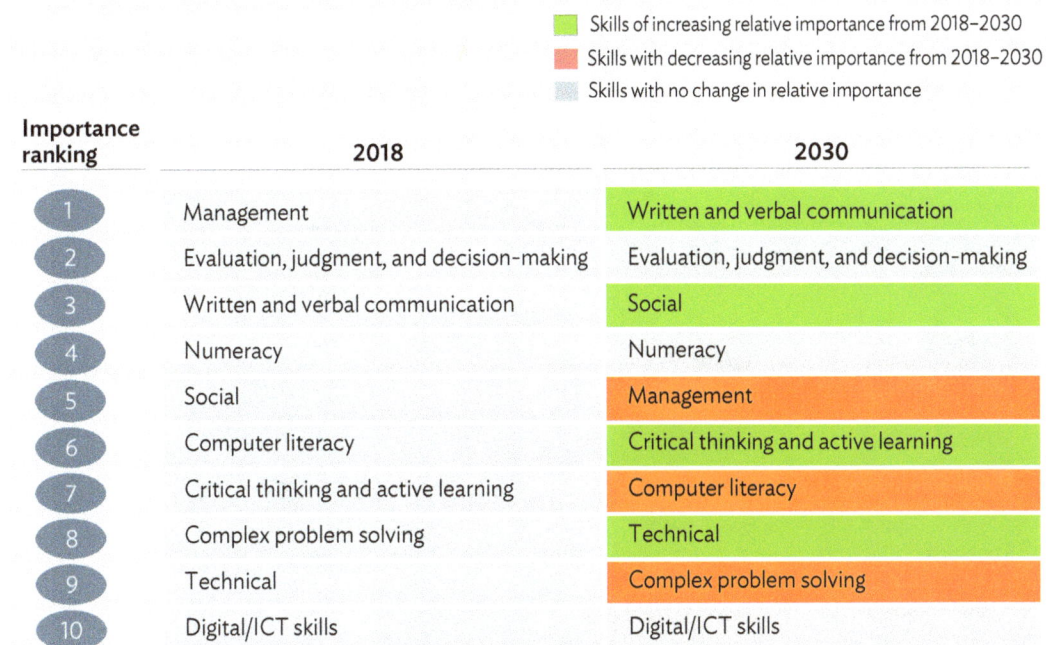

🟩 Skills of increasing relative importance from 2018–2030
🟧 Skills with decreasing relative importance from 2018–2030
⬜ Skills with no change in relative importance

Importance ranking	2018	2030
1	Management	Written and verbal communication
2	Evaluation, judgment, and decision-making	Evaluation, judgment, and decision-making
3	Written and verbal communication	Social
4	Numeracy	Numeracy
5	Social	Management
6	Computer literacy	Critical thinking and active learning
7	Critical thinking and active learning	Computer literacy
8	Complex problem solving	Technical
9	Technical	Complex problem solving
10	Digital/ICT skills	Digital/ICT skills

4IR = Industry 4.0 or Fourth Industrial Revolution, GDP = gross domestic product, ILO = International Labour Organization, IMF = International Monetary Fund, ICT = information and communication technology, NIS = National Institute of Statistics, STEP = Systematic Tracking of Exchanges in Procurement.

Sources: Industry employment –NIS, Cambodia Socio-EconomicSurvey (CSES) 2017and ILO; GDP/Output –NIS, McKinsey and IMF Article IV; World Bank STEP survey (proxied with data from the Lao People's Democratic Republic); Employer survey on impact of 4IR on the tourism industry in Cambodia, n= 39+; Job portal data: jobs in the tourism industry scraped from the job portal Pelprek from July to August 2019.

Box 6: Comparison of Insights in the Tourism Industry versus Past Research

This report finds a net positive impact on employment for the tourism industry in Cambodia. However, given the smaller task shifts observed, the overall impact on employment is smaller than for garment manufacturing. These results broadly align with previous research conducted across other Association of Southeast Asian Nations (ASEAN) member states. However, the differences between the employment impact between tourism and garment manufacturing are larger in the current research.

Source: Oxford Economics. 2018. *Technology and the Future of ASEAN Jobs - The Impact of AI on Workers in ASEAN's Six Largest Economies.* https://www.oxfordeconomics.com/recent-releases/dd577680-7297-4677-aa8f-450da197e132.

Figure 22: Impact of 4IR on the Level of Skills Required in Tourism, 2018–2030

Tourism: Skills

Workers in the tourism industry will require advanced communication, social, and evaluation skills under 4IR

Absolute change in percentage of workers requiring skill at level, 2018–2030

Skills	Basic (%)	Intermediate (%)	Advanced (%)	
Critical thinking and active learning	(21.9)	58.5	4.1	>50%
Written and verbal communication	(7.3)	(89.2)	96.8	>10%
Numeracy	(7.8)	(5.1)	12.9	≤10%; ≥-10%
Complex problem solving	(2.1)	97.2	1.7	< -10%
Management	(0.2)	(40.5)	40.7	< -50%
Social	(48.2)	(50.5)	98.9	
Evaluation, judgment, and decision-making	(0.2)	(90.4)	90.6	
Technical	36.3	51.1	10.1	
Computer literacy	(17.9)	56.5	1.7	
Digital/ICT skills	40.3	57.1	1.0	

( ) = negative, 4IR = Industry 4.0 or Fourth Industrial Revolution, GDP = gross domestic product, ILO = International Labour Organization, IMF = International Monetary Fund, NIS = National Institute of Statistics, STEP = Systematic Tracking of Exchanges in Procurement.

Sources: Industry employment –NIS, Cambodia Socio-EconomicSurvey (CSES) 2017and ILO; GDP/Output –NIS, McKinsey and IMF Article IV; World Bank STEP survey (proxied with data from the Lao People's Democratic Republic); Employer survey on impact of 4IR on the tourism industry in Cambodia, n= 39+; Job portal data: jobs in the tourism industry scraped from the job portal Pelprek from July to August 2019.

Skills Supply Trends

Figure 23 shows the breakdown of the additional demand for training that will be required by workers in the tourism industry under 4IR technology adoption. This reflects the volume of training required to bring the tourism workforce in Cambodia from the skills required in 2018 to the level of skills required by 2030, driven only by 4IR technology adoption. Overall, there will need to be 10.2 million additional person trainings by 2030. Compared to garment manufacturing, there is a much larger demand for on-the-job training in tourism. This is driven by the relatively small impacts on employment, meaning fewer workers will be displaced and newly hired. As a result, most workers will remain in their jobs but require significant upskilling. This means that for the tourism industry, the TVET sector may be required to shift focus and play a role in delivering shorter, real-life focused, training modules within the workplace environment, be it through online and remote learning techniques or by providing in-house trainers to companies.

Figure 23: Additional Person Trainings Required to Meet Skills Demand Driven by 4IR Adoption in Tourism by Training Channel in 2030

Tourism: Skills

The large majority of demand for training driven by 4IR adoption will likely need to be serviced by "On-the-job" training or short professional training

Millions of person trainings required by channel[a]

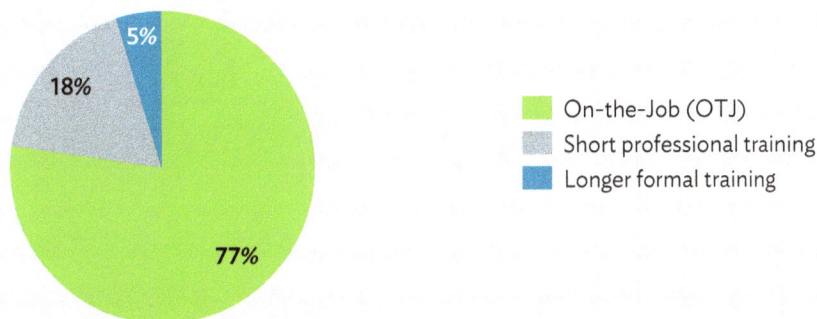

- On-the-Job (OTJ)
- Short professional training
- Longer formal training

4IR = Industry 4.0 or Fourth Industrial Revolution, GDP = gross domestic product, ILO = International Labour Organization, IMF = International Monetary Fund, NIS = National Institute of Statistics, STEP = Systematic Tracking of Exchanges in Procurement.

Notes:
1. Figures include rounding adjustments.
2. One person training refers to training one worker, in one skill from the level required by his occupation's skill profile in 2018 to the relevant level given by the skills profile in 2030.

[a] "On-the-job" training refers to training conducted during day to day such as senior staff instructing junior staff or running internal seminars; "Short professional" training refers to short (between 1 day to 6 months) courses conducted by professional internal or external instructors (e.g. weekend seminars, boot-camps); "Longer formal" trainings refer to trainings longer than 6 months for which workers would likely have to take leave from their jobs, these include returning into formal education such as obtaining a degree.

Sources: Industry employment –NIS, Cambodia Socio-EconomicSurvey (CSES) 2017and ILO; GDP/Output –NIS, McKinsey and IMF Article IV; World Bank STEP survey (proxied with data from the Lao People's Democratic Republic); Employer survey on impact of 4IR on the tourism industry in Cambodia, n= 39+; Job portal data: jobs in the tourism industry scraped from the job portal Pelprek from July to August 2019.

Employers' opinions about the availability of qualified graduates to fill entry-level roles do not differ too much from those in garment manufacturing, raising concerns about the general quality of the TVET sector (Figure 24). Of the surveyed employers, 49% agreed that there is a sufficiently large volume of graduates to meet their company's entry-level hiring needs; however, only 21% agreed that graduates were adequately prepared for entry-level jobs. Compared to findings in the garment manufacturing industry, it appears that a lack of general rather than job-specific skills is the main problem as 61% of employers disagreed or strongly disagreed that graduates have the right level of general skills for entry-level roles.

Figure 24: Employer Sentiment Toward Graduates Hired in the Past 24 Months in Tourism

Tourism: Supply

Employers in the tourism industry are concerned about the lack of preparedness of graduates and the large variance in quality

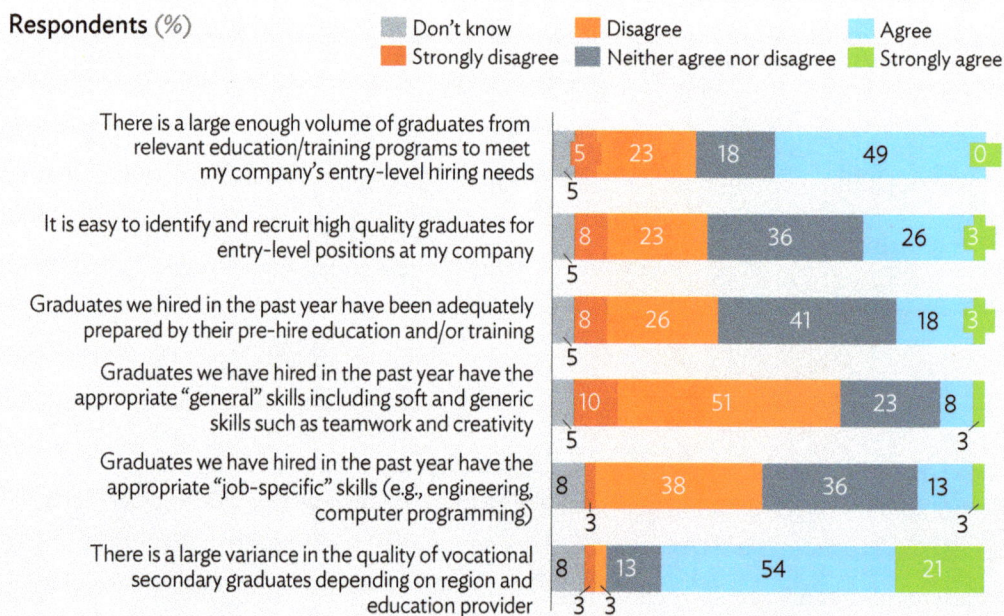

Respondents (%)

Don't know | Disagree | Agree
Strongly disagree | Neither agree nor disagree | Strongly agree

Statement	Strongly disagree	Disagree	Don't know	Neither agree nor disagree	Agree	Strongly agree
There is a large enough volume of graduates from relevant education/training programs to meet my company's entry-level hiring needs	5	23	5	18	49	0
It is easy to identify and recruit high quality graduates for entry-level positions at my company	8	23	5	36	26	3
Graduates we hired in the past year have been adequately prepared by their pre-hire education and/or training	8	26	5	41	18	3
Graduates we have hired in the past year have the appropriate "general" skills including soft and generic skills such as teamwork and creativity	10	51	5	23	8	3
Graduates we have hired in the past year have the appropriate "job-specific" skills (e.g., engineering, computer programming)	8	38	3	36	13	3
There is a large variance in the quality of vocational secondary graduates depending on region and education provider	8	3	3	13	54	21

4IR = Industry 4.0 or Fourth Industrial Revolution, GDP = gross domestic product, ILO = International Labour Organization, IMF = International Monetary Fund, NIS = National Institute of Statistics, STEP = Systematic Tracking of Exchanges in Procurement.

Source: Employer survey on impact of 4IR on the tourism industry in Cambodia, n=40.

CHAPTER 2

Overview of the Training Landscape

This chapter provides insights into the performance of the technical vocational education and training (TVET) sector in Cambodia as it is preparing to deal with the challenges emerging from Industry 4.0 (4IR) technology adoption. The insights are drawn from a survey of training institutions in Cambodia, complemented with insights from the employer surveys discussed in Chapter 1.

There is reasonable alignment between the skills that training institutions believe will be particularly important for 4IR and the perceptions of employers in the garment and tourism industries, which is encouraging. However, some training institutions may be struggling to keep pace with the rate of change in skills demand. For example, 66% of training institutions surveyed review and update their curricula on a less than annual basis, and only 30% of training time is spent on workplace-based training, which are below international benchmarks for TVET.

While there appears to be frequent engagement between training institutes and industry, the quality of workers produced appears to be lacking, which is a cause for concern. There seems to be a severe misalignment between training institutions and employers in their perception of graduates' preparedness for work, including skills required to perform well in entry-level roles, as well as general and job-specific skills. While 59% of training institutions in Cambodia believe graduates are well prepared for entry-level positions, only 10% of employers in garment manufacturing and 21% of employers in tourism agreed with this perception.

A survey of 51 training institutions was commissioned to better understand the supply of talent and skills for the adoption of 4IR technology in Cambodia. Majority of the respondents are TVET institutes, equally split across the private and public sectors. On average, only 27% of the funding for the training institutions surveyed originates from public sources. Institutions of different sizes were sampled, with almost 90% of the respondents training from 200 to 10,000 students annually. More than 40% offer courses on jobs related to construction, and more than 30% provide courses on education, financial and professional services, hotels and tourism, hospitality, and mechanical and electrical engineering.

Industry 4.0 Readiness

Insights from training institutions paint a very different picture compared to the employer surveys. An overwhelming majority of institutions feel well prepared for 4IR (Figure 25). For example, almost 73% of training institutions surveyed believe they have a good understanding of the skills that need to be developed to prepare graduates for employment along with the adoption of 4IR technologies. Further, 56% claim to have dedicated programs related to 4IR skills, with 71% planning to develop or expand such programs by 2025. While 56% of these institutions agree or strongly agree that they will be able to adequately prepare their graduates as per their ongoing plans, 62% also agreed or strongly agreed with the statement that they need additional financial and technical support, specifically for dealing with 4IR skill training.

Figure 25: Perception of Training Institutions on 4IR Readiness in Tourism

Training Sector: 4IR readiness

Training institutions generally feel well equipped for 4IR, however 62% will require some additional support

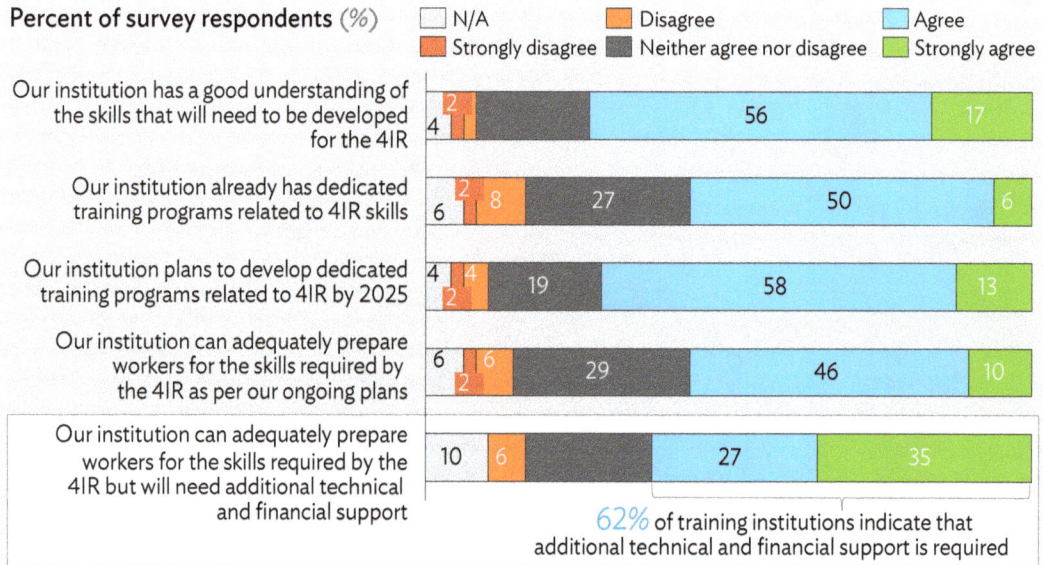

Percent of survey respondents (%)

☐ N/A	☐ Disagree	☐ Agree
☐ Strongly disagree	☐ Neither agree nor disagree	☐ Strongly agree

Our institution has a good understanding of the skills that will need to be developed for the 4IR: 2 | 4 | 56 | 17

Our institution already has dedicated training programs related to 4IR skills: 2 | 8 | 6 | 27 | 50 | 6

Our institution plans to develop dedicated training programs related to 4IR by 2025: 4 | 4 | 2 | 19 | 58 | 13

Our institution can adequately prepare workers for the skills required by the 4IR as per our ongoing plans: 6 | 6 | 2 | 29 | 46 | 10

Our institution can adequately prepare workers for the skills required by the 4IR but will need additional technical and financial support: 10 | 6 | 27 | 35

62% of training institutions indicate that additional technical and financial support is required

4IR = Industry 4.0 or Fourth Industrial Revolution, N/A = not applicable.

Source: Training institution survey on impact of 4IR in Cambodia; n = 48.

There is generally good alignment between the skills that training institutes believe will become more important under 4IR and the skills that employers (in the garment manufacturing and tourism industries) believe will become more important (Figure 26). The skill category most training institutions deem to become much more important over the next 5 years due to 4IR is evaluation and critical thinking, which indicates their increasing importance in both industries. This is closely followed by complex problem solving and digital and information and communication technology skills. Notably, employers in tourism believe digital skills to be much more important compared to employers in garment manufacturing and even training institutions.

Curriculum

Aligning curricula with actual industry needs is one of the most important but often most challenging component of an effective training and education sector. It relies on frequent updating and close communication with industry, given the speed of change in 4IR technologies in the workplace. Regular curriculum reviews are therefore critical to keep pace with the skill changes related to 4IR. However, 66% of training institutions surveyed review and update their curricula less than annually (Figure 27).

Figure 26: Potential Impact of 4IR on Importance of Different Skills in Tourism Over the Next 5 Years

Training Sector: 4IR readiness

Training institutions, as opposed to employers, believe evaluation, critical thinking, and problem solving will be more important than digital skills for 4IR

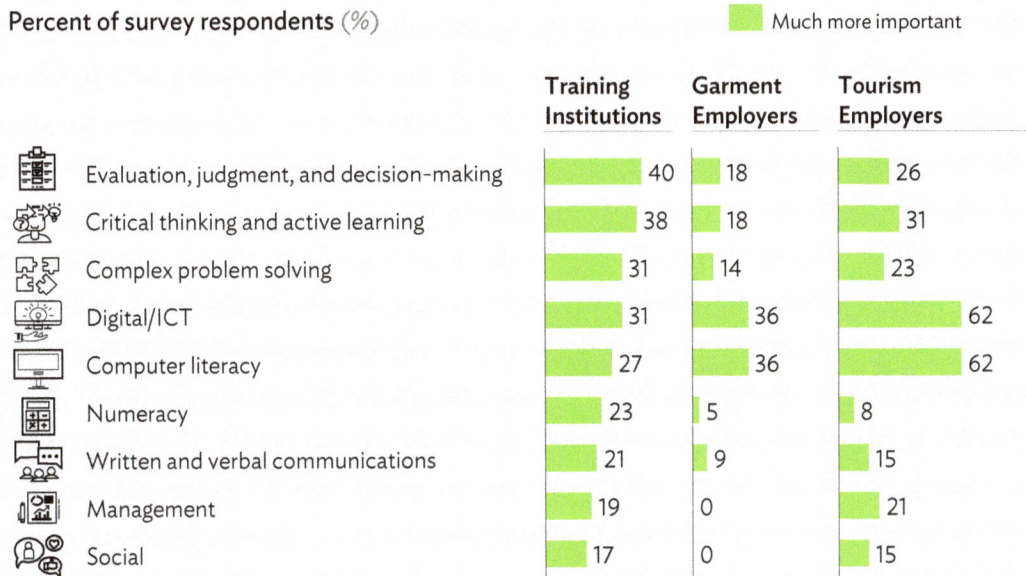

Percent of survey respondents (%)   Much more important

	Training Institutions	Garment Employers	Tourism Employers
Evaluation, judgment, and decision-making	40	18	26
Critical thinking and active learning	38	18	31
Complex problem solving	31	14	23
Digital/ICT	31	36	62
Computer literacy	27	36	62
Numeracy	23	5	8
Written and verbal communications	21	9	15
Management	19	0	21
Social	17	0	15

4IR = Industry 4.0 or Fourth Industrial Revolution, ICT = information and communication technology.

Source: Training institution survey on impact of 4IR in Cambodia, n = 48; Employer survey on impact of 4IR on the garment manufacturing industry in Cambodia, n = 22; Employer survey on impact of 4IR on the tourism industry in Cambodia, n = 39.

Figure 27: Frequency of Review and Update of Curricula by Training Institutions

Training Sector: Curriculum

66% of all training institutions review and update their curricula less than once a year

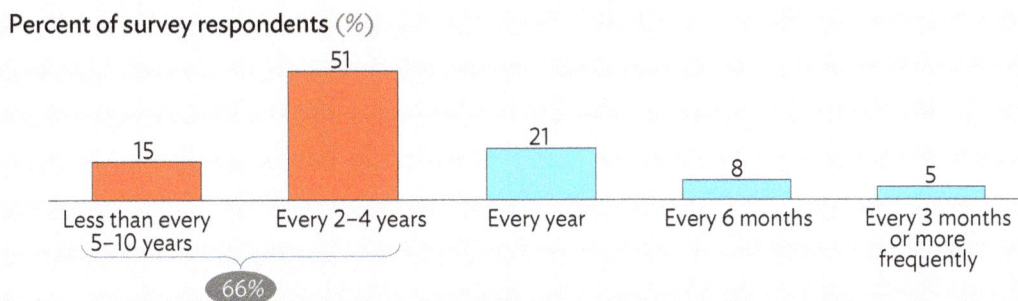

Percent of survey respondents (%)

Less than every 5–10 years	Every 2–4 years	Every year	Every 6 months	Every 3 months or more frequently
15	51	21	8	5

66%

4IR = Industry 4.0 or Fourth Industrial Revolution.

Source: Training institution survey on impact of 4IR in Cambodia; n = 39.

Figure 28: Share of Curriculum Time Spent by Type of Training

Training Sector: Curriculum

There is a lower focus on workplace/practical training than is seen in leading international vocational programs

Average percentage share of total time spent on training type at surveyed institutions (%)

According to OECD research, more than three-quarters of vocational training programmes in Denmark, Germany, Finland, France, Norway, and Switzerland at the upper secondary level spend 50%–75% of instructional time in practical or on-site training.

4IR = Industry 4.0 or Fourth Industrial Revolution, OECD = Organisation for Economic Co-operation and Development.

Note: "Theoretical" training refers to lectures, "Project-based" refers to student projects and "Workplace-based" refers to on-the-job training such as industry apprenticeships.

Source: Training institution survey on impact of 4IR in Cambodia; n = 39; M. Kuczera. 2010. Learning for Jobs—The OECD International Survey of VET Systems: First Results and Technical Report OECD.

Another aspect to consider is the content of the curriculum. Evidence from Indonesia suggests that on-the-job training and hands-on learning are cited among the top three most effective instructional techniques according to vocational students.[25] Countries such as Denmark, Finland, France, Germany, Norway, and Switzerland spend 50%–75% of instructional time at the upper secondary level on practical or on-site training.[26] In Cambodia, only 27% of time during training is spent workplace-based and 25% on classroom-based student projects with almost half of time being allocated to theoretical work (Figure 28).

In line with the earlier claim that training institutes are already offering 4IR training, many Cambodian training institutions surveyed provide courses relevant to 4IR, and the adoption of at least basic digital technologies in the classroom is also encouraging (Figure 29). Of the those surveyed, 54% stated that they have rolled out courses specifically focusing on 4IR,[27] 72% are already running digital programs

[25]   Asia Philanthropy Circle. 2017. *Catalysing Productive Livelihood: A Guide to Education Interventions with an Accelerated Path to Scale and Impact.* https://www.edumap-indonesia.asiaphilanthropycircle.org/.

[26]   Organisation for Economic Co-operation and Development (OECD). 2010. *Learning for jobs—The OECD International Survey of VET Systems: First Results and Technical Report.* https://www.oecd.org/education/skills-beyond-school/47334855.pdf.

[27]   Compared to the questions asked for Figure 11, this portion of the survey focused specifically on the hands-on use of technology in the classroom. Survey respondents were asked whether their training institution already offers new courses specifically for 4IR technologies (e.g., educating on the use of 4IR technologies in specific industry sectors). Some institutions may have dedicated training programs related to 4IR skills, which could be soft skills (Figure 25), but have not gone as far as focus on the use of 4IR technology/machines in courses (e.g., training students to work with or operate robotic manufacturing assistants, or having such technology available for students). Hence, this more nuanced question was included in the survey.

Figure 29: Prevalence of Technology-Related Courses and Technology-Based Delivery in Teaching at Training Institutions

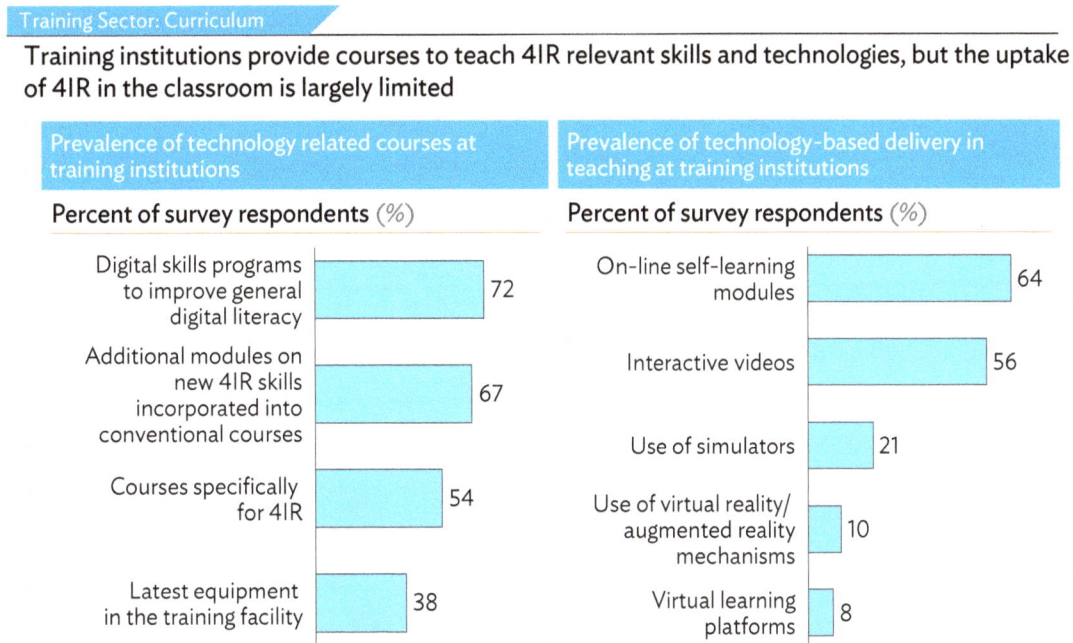

Training Sector: Curriculum

Training institutions provide courses to teach 4IR relevant skills and technologies, but the uptake of 4IR in the classroom is largely limited

Prevalence of technology related courses at training institutions	Prevalence of technology-based delivery in teaching at training institutions
Percent of survey respondents (%)	Percent of survey respondents (%)

Prevalence of technology related courses at training institutions — Percent of survey respondents (%):

- Digital skills programs to improve general digital literacy: 72
- Additional modules on new 4IR skills incorporated into conventional courses: 67
- Courses specifically for 4IR: 54
- Latest equipment in the training facility: 38

Prevalence of technology-based delivery in teaching at training institutions — Percent of survey respondents (%):

- On-line self-learning modules: 64
- Interactive videos: 56
- Use of simulators: 21
- Use of virtual reality/augmented reality mechanisms: 10
- Virtual learning platforms: 8

4IR = Industry 4.0 or Fourth Industrial Revolution.

Source: Training institution survey on impact of 4IR in Cambodia; n = 32.

at improving digital literacy, and 67% have incorporated additional modules on 4IR-relevant skills into their conventional courses. When it comes to technology adoption in the classroom, some technologies are heavily favored. Already 64% of institutions make use of online self-learning tools and 56% use interactive videos, but only 21% are employing some form of simulators for technical training; and only 10% or less are using virtual or augmented reality and virtual learning platforms. Since the latter technologies are more nascent and expensive, the limited uptake is likely linked to a lack of information about the latest applications and/or financial constraints.

Many training institutions surveyed also engage in a range of programs and activities in addition to training courses that are aimed at providing students with better information and access to career opportunities and support (Figure 30). For example, on the career front, 82% receive visits from company representatives and 79% arrange meetings with career coaches or visits and field trips to companies. Of those surveyed, 79% also help with curriculum vitae or resume preparation.

There is some room for improvement as only half of the institutions provide information on job market conditions (i.e., wages and job prospects in different industries), or employment performance (including wages and jobs) of alumni. Only 46% say they provide noncareer advice to students such as counseling on personal or financial matters.

Figure 30: Programs Provided in Addition to Training Courses

Training Sector: Curriculum

Training institutions appear to be actively exposing students to industry, but could improve on information provision and noncareer support

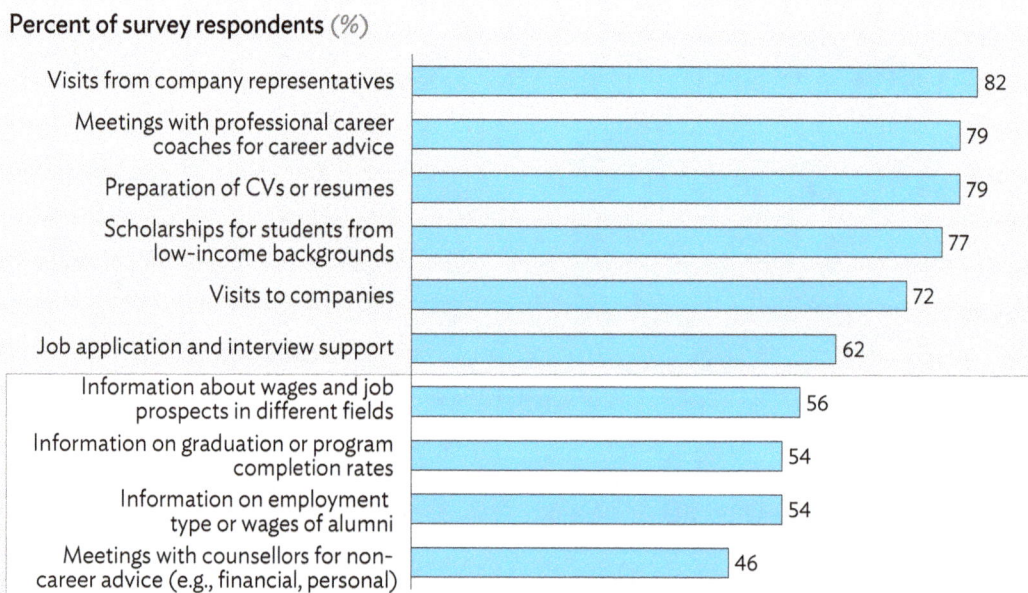

Percent of survey respondents (%)

Visits from company representatives	82
Meetings with professional career coaches for career advice	79
Preparation of CVs or resumes	79
Scholarships for students from low-income backgrounds	77
Visits to companies	72
Job application and interview support	62
Information about wages and job prospects in different fields	56
Information on graduation or program completion rates	54
Information on employment type or wages of alumni	54
Meetings with counsellors for non-career advice (e.g., financial, personal)	46

4IR = Industry 4.0 or Fourth Industrial Revolution, CV = curriculum vitae.

Source: Training institution survey on impact of 4IR in Cambodia; n = 39.

Industry Engagement

Training institutions surveyed displayed very positive levels of interaction with potential employers, in contrast to anecdotal evidence from targeted interviews with training institutions and from in-country consultation workshops. Of those surveyed, 86% said they communicate and coordinate with employers in relevant industries several times a year (Figure 31).

Workplace-based training is the most commonly reported form of engagement with industry (Figure 32). Other activities include working with employers to organize job fairs to advertise opportunities, gathering inputs from industry on curriculum design, and collaborating on apprenticeships. There is a lack of employer-led interaction such as provision of equipment, train-the-teacher programs, and teaching placements.

While training institutions appear to engage with employers actively, active engagement from employers seems to vary by industry (Figure 33). The tourism industry appears to be somewhat active in engaging with the training and education sector. For example, over a quarter of employers in the tourism industry claim to work with training providers to determine what courses should be offered, and provide equipment and facilities for students to receive hands-on training. Only 5% of employers in garment

Figure 31: Frequency of Communication with Employers in Relevant Sectors by Training Institutions

Training Sector: Employers

86% of training institutions communicate with employers at least two times a year

Percent of survey respondents (%)

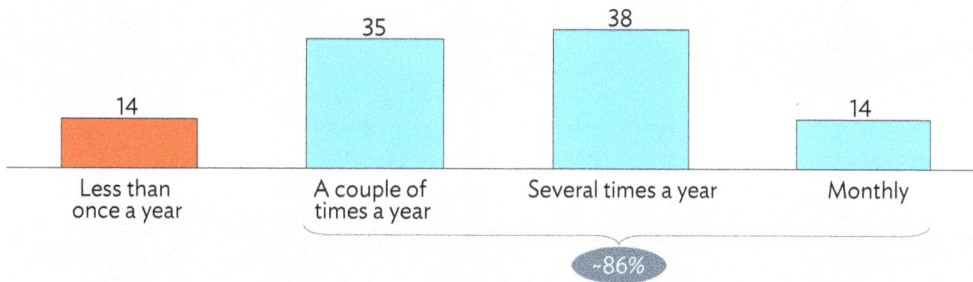

Note: May not add up to 100% due to rounding.
Source: Training institution survey on impact of Industry 4.0 in Cambodia; n = 37.

Figure 32: Potential Partnerships and Engagement between Industry and Training Sector

Training Sector: Employers

While most training institutions engage employers, few are able to get access to industry equipment or industry training for their teaching staff

Percent of surveyed training institutions (%)

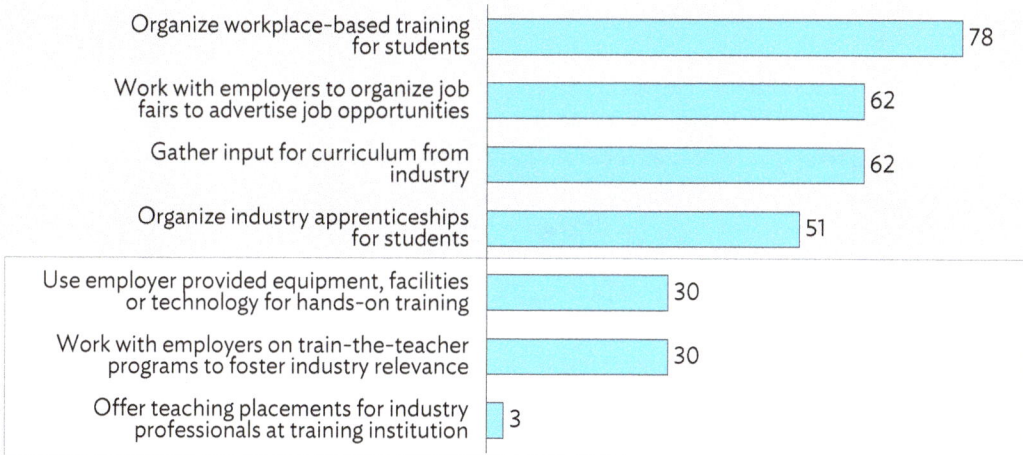

Source: Training institution survey on impact of Industry 4.0 in Cambodia; n = 37.

Figure 33: Potential Partnerships and Engagement between Industry and Training Sector

Training Sector: Employers

The tourism industry is more active in engaging training institutions but both industries appear willing to explore sharing equipment for training

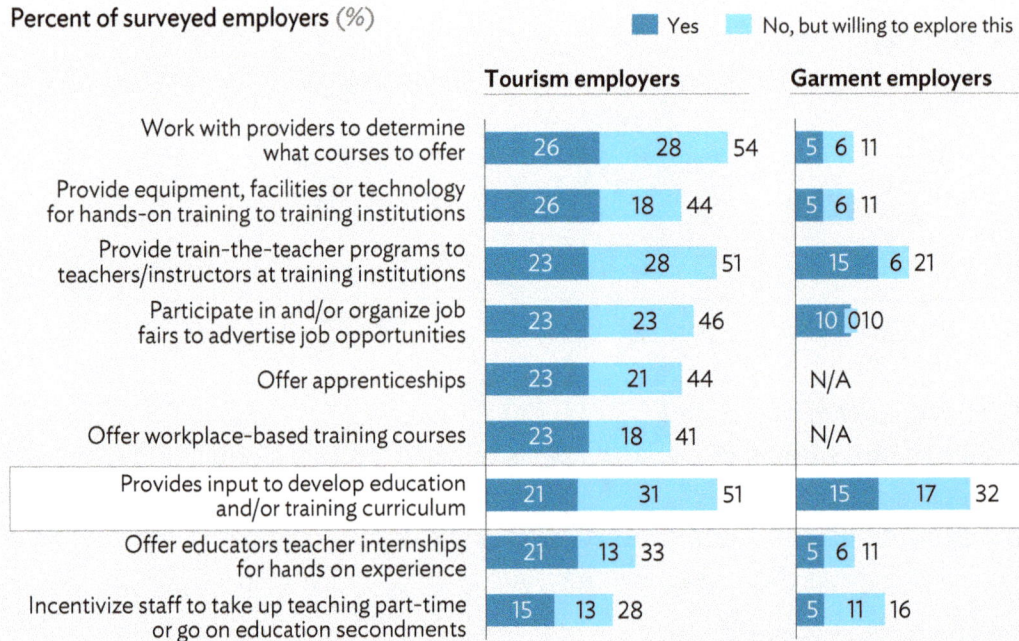

Percent of surveyed employers (%)

■ Yes   ■ No, but willing to explore this

	Tourism employers			Garment employers		
Work with providers to determine what courses to offer	26	28	54	5	6	11
Provide equipment, facilities or technology for hands-on training to training institutions	26	18	44	5	6	11
Provide train-the-teacher programs to teachers/instructors at training institutions	23	28	51	15	6	21
Participate in and/or organize job fairs to advertise job opportunities	23	23	46	10	0	10
Offer apprenticeships	23	21	44		N/A	
Offer workplace-based training courses	23	18	41		N/A	
Provides input to develop education and/or training curriculum	21	31	51	15	17	32
Offer educators teacher internships for hands on experience	21	13	33	5	6	11
Incentivize staff to take up teaching part-time or go on education secondments	15	13	28	5	11	16

4IR = Industry 4.0 or Fourth Industrial Revolution, N/A = not applicable.

Source: Employer survey on impact of 4IR on the garment manufacturing industry in Cambodia, n = 20; Employer survey on impact of 4IR on the tourism industry in Cambodia, n = 39.

manufacturing do so. Notably, employers across both industries appear to be willing to provide input on curricula despite training institutions reportedly engaging employers not as frequently. There appears to be a missed opportunity to improve coordination between the training sector and industry.

Data from the employer survey further indicate a severe lack of training for workers in both industries. Only 5% of employers in garment manufacturing and 31% of employers in tourism agree or strongly agree with the statement that most of their staff have received training in the past 12 months. While the tourism industry partially makes up for this by providing on-the-job training, the garment manufacturing industry also provides little of it. (Figure 34).

Teachers, Trainers, and Instructors

It is encouraging to see that many training institutions are actively engaged in professional development and performance assessment of their teaching and training staff, with 89% of those surveyed giving formal annual/semiannual performance reviews and 73% providing frequent feedback (Figure 35).

Figure 34: Current Annual Training Received while in Employment in Garment Manufacturing and Tourism by Training Channel

The tourism industry is very active in on-the-job training but provides limited formal training to workers

Training required by channel, days per year   Type of training   On-the-Job   Formal mid-career

Occupation	Garment industry		Tourism industry	
	On-the-Job	Formal	On-the-Job	Formal
Managerial	3	3	6	2
Administrative	2	2	5	2
Technical	4	5	5	3
Manual job	4	1	7	3
Customer-facing	4	4	9	3

4IR = Industry 4.0 or Fourth Industrial Revolution.

Source: Employer survey on impact of 4IR on the garment manufacturing industry in Cambodia, n = 20; Employer survey on impact of 4IR on the tourism industry in Cambodia, n = 39.

Figure 35: Practices in Support of Instructors and Teaching Staff of Training Institutions

Most training institutions do not allocate designated on-the-job time for staff to gain new practical knowledge and teaching techniques

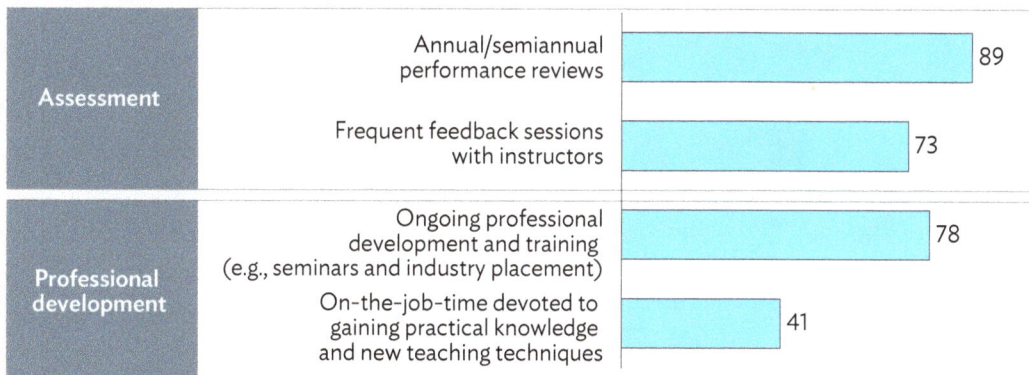

Assessment		
Annual/semiannual performance reviews		89
Frequent feedback sessions with instructors		73

Professional development		
Ongoing professional development and training (e.g., seminars and industry placement)		78
On-the-job-time devoted to gaining practical knowledge and new teaching techniques		41

Source: Training institution survey on impact of Industry 4.0 in Cambodia; n = 37.

Of those surveyed, 78% provide ongoing professional development and industry relevant training (e.g., industry seminars and industry exposure) for instructors, but only 41% allow instructors to devote time during working hours to pursue ways to refresh their practical knowledge and/or learn new techniques on their own.

Performance and Policy Support

Of training institutions surveyed, 43% said they face little difficulty in filling up student spots and vacancies across their courses (Figure 36). For those who do, the key reasons for these difficulties appear to be related to lack of price competitiveness, the inability of trainees to differentiate programs, and a lack of awareness among trainees about programs offered.

Training institutions are largely satisfied with the effectiveness of public policy (Figure 37). For example, 89% of institutions surveyed believe that government inspection and certification processes that assess the quality of education institutions have a positive or strongly positive impact. In terms of future policy priorities, establishing strong quality assurance as well as support mechanisms for industry collaboration are considered by those surveyed to be among the most impactful policies (Figure 38).

Figure 36: Reasons for Difficulty in filling up Student Spots or Vacancies at Training Institutions

Training Sector: Policy

43% of training institutions find it difficult to fill vacancies, largely due to lack of price competitiveness and insufficient information about training

Percent of survey respondents (%)

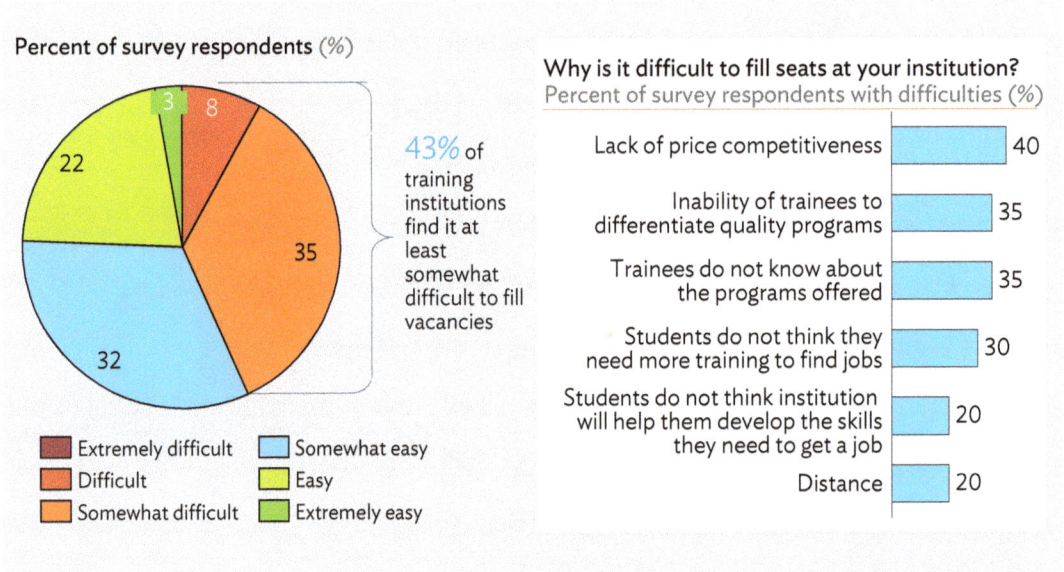

43% of training institutions find it at least somewhat difficult to fill vacancies

- Extremely difficult
- Difficult
- Somewhat difficult
- Somewhat easy
- Easy
- Extremely easy

Why is it difficult to fill seats at your institution?
Percent of survey respondents with difficulties (%)

Lack of price competitiveness	40
Inability of trainees to differentiate quality programs	35
Trainees do not know about the programs offered	35
Students do not think they need more training to find jobs	30
Students do not think institution will help them develop the skills they need to get a job	20
Distance	20

Source: Training institution survey on impact of Industry 4.0 in Cambodia; n = 20.

Figure 37: Perception of Policy Effectiveness by Training Institutions

Training Sector: Policy

Training institutions deem government policy as mostly effective, however, a significant amount of respondents is not aware of its impact

Percent of survey respondents (%)

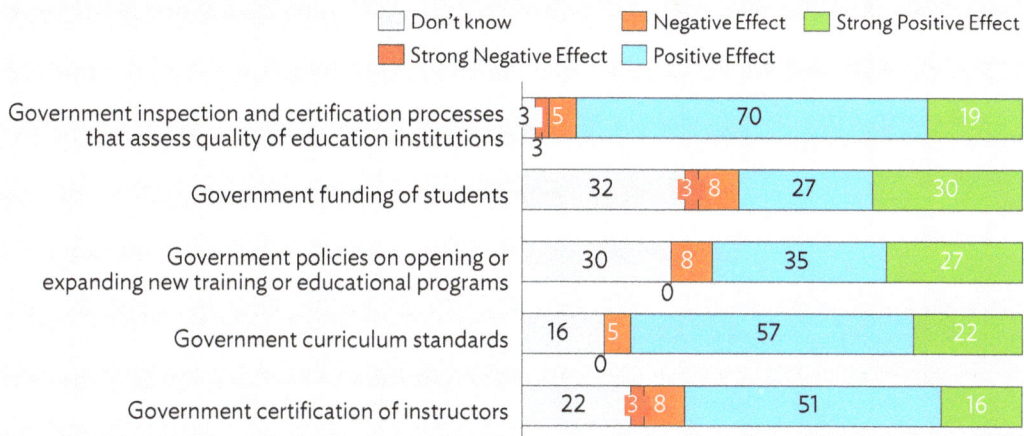

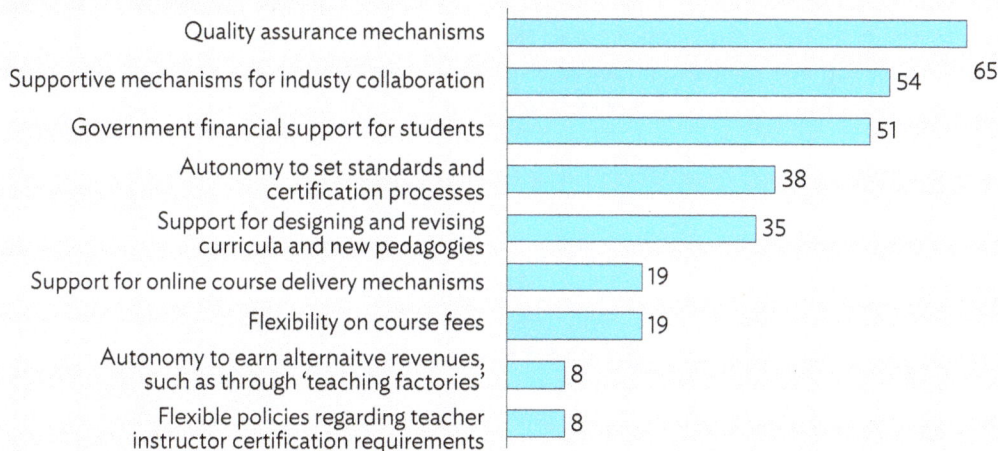

Legend: Don't know | Negative Effect | Strong Positive Effect | Strong Negative Effect | Positive Effect

Policy	Don't know	Strong Neg	Neg	Positive	Strong Positive
Government inspection and certification processes that assess quality of education institutions	3	3	5	70	19
Government funding of students	32	3	8	27	30
Government policies on opening or expanding new training or educational programs	30	0	8	35	27
Government curriculum standards	16	0	5	57	22
Government certification of instructors	22	3	8	51	16

Source: Training institution survey on impact of Industry 4.0 in Cambodia; n = 37.

Figure 38: Perspective on Most Impactful Public Policies on Training Provision

Training Sector: Policy

Training institutions believe that quality assurance, supporting industry collaboration and financial support are most the helpful policies

Percent of survey respondents (%)

Policy	%
Quality assurance mechanisms	65
Supportive mechanisms for industy collaboration	54
Government financial support for students	51
Autonomy to set standards and certification processes	38
Support for designing and revising curricula and new pedagogies	35
Support for online course delivery mechanisms	19
Flexibility on course fees	19
Autonomy to earn alternaitve revenues, such as through 'teaching factories'	8
Flexible policies regarding teacher instructor certification requirements	8

Source: Training institution survey on impact of Industry 4.0 in Cambodia; n = 37.

Supply and Demand Mismatches

According to the training institutions surveyed, the most common reason why graduates may not be able to find a job is a lack of job opportunities and that their certifications are not well recognized by employers (Figure 39).

Figure 39: Reasons for Students Unable to Find Employment Upon Graduation by Prevalence

Training Sector: Students

Training institutions believe a lack of job opportunities, certification recognition, and preparation for jobs are key employment barriers

Ranking score, 1–Most common; 5–Least common

Rank		Average Ranking
1	Not enough job opportunities	2.0
2	Graduates' certifications are not well-recognized by employers	2.9
3	Education and training programs do not adequately prepare job seekers for job opportunities	3.1
4	Not enough opportunities for job seekers to complete relevant education or training for job opportunities	3.6
5	Enough jobs, but students unaware of job opportunities	3.6

Source: Training institution survey on impact of Industry 4.0 in Cambodia; n = 39.

There appears to be a severe misalignment between training institutions and employers in their perception of graduates' preparedness for work, including skills required to perform well in entry-level roles, as well as general and job-specific skills (Figure 40). For example, while 59% of training institutes surveyed believe that graduates are adequately well prepared for entry-level positions, only 10% of employers in tourism and 21% of employers in garment manufacturing agree.

Increasing the quality of engagement between employers and training institutions on curriculum (as earlier noted) can potentially address this significant mismatch in skill expectations between employers and training institutions. Survey results suggest that while training institutions may have a good understanding of the skill categories of rising importance for 4IR, the actual implementation of skill training, or depth and specific type of skills taught, do not match industry requirements. There are also opportunities to improve teacher development to help close this skills gap. As highlighted earlier, only 41% of institutions allow instructors to devote time during working hours to pursue ways to refresh their practical knowledge and/or learn new techniques on their own.

Figure 40: Perception of Preparedness of Graduates for Entry-Level Positions

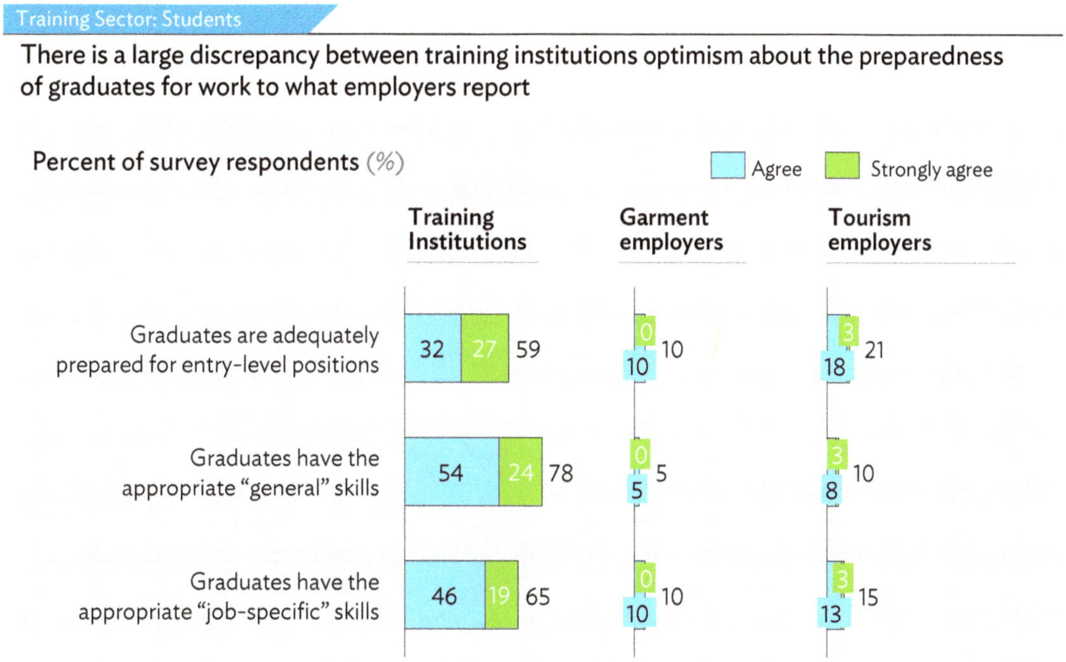

4IR = Industry 4.0 or Fourth Industrial Revolution.

Source: Training institution survey on impact of 4IR in Cambodia, n = 37; Employer survey on impact of 4IR on the garment manufacturing industry in Cambodia, n = 20; Employer survey on impact of 4IR on the tourism industry in Cambodia, n = 39.

CHAPTER 3
National Policy Responses

A thorough scan of all ongoing policies and programs by the government, industry, and civil society in Cambodia reveal a range of strategies that seek to improve the readiness of the national workforce for Industry 4.0 (4IR). Some focus has been placed on stimulating higher technology adoption by firms (largely through start-up creation efforts), building awareness of "in-demand" jobs and skills, fostering government–industry–civil society collaboration, and building more inclusive models for skills development. However, there appears to be weak focus on a number of critical policy areas. Limited focus has been demonstrated in the areas of creating incentives for skills development, establishing lifelong learning models, ensuring the relevance and agility of education and training curricula to emerging skill needs, encouraging a focus on skills, and creating social protection mechanisms for the emerging class of gig economy workers. While the Government of Cambodia appears to have developed a clear 4IR vision in its recently launched Trade Strategy (2019–2023), there is room to improve overall integration with national skills strategies, stronger coordination between government ministries and levels, as well as alignment between industry and training institutions.

The policy assessment leverages a combination of government policy documents relevant to 4IR and skills, academic literature on Cambodia's skills development, and reviews of government policies, as well as relevant local surveys. These sources have been referenced throughout the write-up.

Overview of the 4IR Policy Landscape

Though still a nascent concept, awareness of the potential that 4IR has for socioeconomic progress has been increasing in the government.[28] Acknowledging that most of the country's industry sectors have not experienced the Third Industrial Revolution (referring to the deployment of basic automation technologies), the government sees "an opportunity to leapfrog in stages toward 4IR" through a two-pronged strategy: leveraging foreign demand and technology transfer, and strengthening its physical and digital infrastructure.[29]

---

[28] This is discussed in a number of media articles, including: S. Chan. 2018. Adapting to Industry 4.0 a top priority: Ministry. *Khmer Times*. 4 September. https://www.khmertimeskh.com/529898/adapting-to-industry-4-0-a-top-priority-ministry/; R. Spiess. 2019. Ready for a (digital) revolution? *Southeast Asia Global*. 28 March. https://southeastasiaglobe.com/cambodia-ready-for-a-digital-revolution/; and V. Dara. 2019. Help Requested for Industry 4.0 Labour. *The Phnom Penh Post*. 17 June. https://www.phnompenhpost.com/national/help-requested-industry-40-labour.

[29] Government of Cambodia, Ministry of Commerce. 2019. *Cambodia Trade Integration Strategy 2019–2023*. https://www.moc.gov.kh/Portals/0/Docs/OfficialDocs/CTIS-20190725143301726.pdf.

While a robust approach for 4IR has not yet been applied, a variety of national policy and strategy documents—both developed and in progress—reflects an intention to strengthen the country's capacity for 4IR technology adoption. These include:

(i) **Cambodia Trade Integration Strategy 2019–2023**. This is the first national document that comprehensively sets out the national strategy for 4IR (footnote 29). It was released in July 2019 by an inter-ministerial taskforce with contributions by multilateral organizations including the United Nations Development Program, United Nations Conference on Trade and Development, and the World Trade Organization.

(ii) **Rectangular Strategy Phase IV.** This national strategy document sets the socioeconomic vision for the country, and reflects "readiness for the digital economy and the Fourth Industrial Revolution" as one of the four priorities for economic diversification and new sources of growth.[30]

(iii) **Industrial Development Policy 2015–2025**. Though 4IR is not explicitly referenced, this policy lists "digitalization" as one of the four pillars of industrial policy. [31]

(iv) **National Technical and Vocational Education and Training Policy 2017–2025**. Supported by an Asian Development Bank (ADB) grant and managed by the Directorate-General of Technical and Vocational Education and Training (DG-TVET) under the Ministry of Labor and Vocational Training (MLVT), this policy guides national skills development strategies, placing emphasis on improving trainer quality, pedagogy, and learning resources in response to current technology development.[32]

(v) **Cambodian Information and Communications Technology (ICT) Master Plan 2020.** This is currently being supported by a working committee formed by the Ministry of Economy and Finance (MEF), the Ministry of Post and Telecommunications, the Ministry of Commerce, Ministry of Information, and the Council for the Development of Cambodia. Five priority projects have been identified for the plan, which include an e-government framework, cybersecurity, e-education, e-commerce, and e-tourism.[33]

(vi) **Cambodia Digital Economy Policy (in progress).** Led by a technical committee established within the Supreme National Economic Council under the MEF, this policy will set out strategies to achieve the country's vision of becoming a predominantly digital economy by 2023, and is aimed to be finalized by July 2020.[34] The World Bank has provided support for this policy in its 2018 study, which conducted a landscape scan of current digital policies and adoption levels in the nation, and recommended priority areas for the policy.[35]

(vii) **Garment and Footwear Sector Development Strategy 2019–2025 (in progress)** by the MEF.[36] This will include a focus on shifting the sector to higher skill and value-added activities through the adoption of new technologies and upskilling, and was expected to be released by the end of 2019.[37]

---

[30] Government of Cambodia. 2018. *Rectangular Strategy for Growth, Employment, Equity, and Efficiency: Building the Foundation Toward Realizing the Cambodia Vision 2050 Phase IV.* http://cnv.org.kh/wp-content/uploads/2012/10/Rectangular-Strategy-Phase-IV-of-the-Royal-Government-of-Cambodia-of-the-Sixth-Legislature-of-the-National-Assembly-2018-2023.pdf.

[31] Government of Cambodia. 2015. *Cambodia Industrial Development Policy 2015–2025.* https://www.eurocham-cambodia.org/uploads/97dae-idp_19may15_com_official.pdf.

[32] ADB. 2018. *Cambodia's new Technical and Vocational Education and Training Policy.* https://www.adb.org/sites/default/files/publication/401691/adb-brief-089-cambodia-new-tvet-policy.pdf. Also based on input from engaged national expert Trevor Sworn.

[33] Telecommunications Regulator of Cambodia. 2015. *Cambodian ICT Masterplan 2020.* https://www.trc.gov.kh/summary-on-cambodian-ict-masterplan-2020/. Also based on input from engaged national expert, Trevor Sworn.

[34] Presentation by Kong Marry, advisor to Deputy Prime Minister, Ministry of Economy and Finance, titled "Digital transformation and policy toward Cambodia's digital economy."

[35] World Bank Group. 2018. *Benefiting from the digital economy: Cambodia policy note.* Available at: http://documents.worldbank.org/curated/en/100841543598854492/pdf/128267-REVISED-Digital-Economy-web.pdf.

[36] Government of Cambodia, Ministry of Economy and Finance (MEF). *Cambodia Garment and Textile Strategy.* Provided by the MEF.

[37] Based on consultation with the MEF in July 2019.

(viii) **Productivity Master Plan 2020–2030 (in progress)** by the Ministry of Industry, Science, Technology and Innovation. The plan features 4IR as one of the strategies to promote productivity gains in industries.[38]

In addition to these key strategies and policies, the Council of Ministers in January 2020 approved renaming the Ministry of Industry and Handicraft into the Ministry of Industry, Science, Technology, and Innovation, seen as an important step to enhance the country's preparedness for 4IR.[39] Created to oversee all industry development efforts, the ministry's scope of operations was also revised and now includes a new objective of facilitating the development of scientific and technological research within the context of 4IR, and translate this into practical approaches to industry innovation (footnote 40).

Table 1 summarizes Cambodia's key policies and responses to 4IR, each further expounded in Chapter 4.

Table 1: Key Policies Relevant to Managing the Impact of 4IR on Skills

Policy Document	Responsible Entity	Relevance
Cambodia Trade Integration Strategy 2019–2023	An inter-ministerial taskforce led by the Ministry of Commerce in collaboration with the UNDP, UNCTAD, and WTO	The first national document which comprehensively sets out the national strategy for Industry 4.0 (4IR)
National Technical and Vocational Education and Training Policy 2017-2025	Directorate-General of Technical and Vocational Education and Training (DG-TVET) under the Ministry of Labor and Vocational Training (MLVT), supported by ADB	Guides national skills development strategies
Cambodian Information and Communications Technology (ICT) Master Plan 2020	Working committee comprising Ministry of Economy and Finance (MEF), Ministry of Post and Telecommunications, Ministry of Commerce, Ministry of Information and the Council for the Development of Cambodia	National strategy for ICT development. Priority projects include an e-government framework, cybersecurity, e-education, e-commerce, and e-tourism
Cambodia Digital Economy Policy (in progress)	Ministry of Economy and Finance (MEF), supported by the World Bank	National strategy to achieve Cambodia's vision of becoming a predominantly digital economy by 2023
Establishment of the Ministry of Science, Technology and Innovation	Ministry of Industry, Science, Technology and Innovation (previously known as the Ministry of Industry and Handicrafts)	Name and scope change of the national ministry overseeing all industry development in the country to facilitate domestic scientific and technology research and adoption of 4IR technologies by industry

UNCTAD = United Nations Conference on Trade and Development, UNDP = UN Development Program, WTO = World Trade Organization.

Sources: Government of Cambodia, Ministry of Commerce. 2019. *Cambodia Trade Integration Strategy 2019–2023*. https://www.moc.gov.kh/Portals/0/Docs/OfficialDocs/CTIS-20190725143301726.pdf; ADB. 2018. *Cambodia's new Technical and Vocational Education and Training Policy*. https://www.adb.org/sites/default/files/publication/401691/adb-brief-089-cambodia-new-tvet-policy.pdf; Telecommunications Regulator of Cambodia. 2015. *Cambodian ICT Masterplan 2020*. https://www.trc.gov.kh/4252/; and presentation by M. Kong, advisor to Deputy Prime Minister, MEF, titled "Digital transformation and policy toward Cambodia's digital economy."

---

[38] Based on the consultation with the Ministry of Industry and Handicrafts in July 2019, now renamed Ministry of Industry, Science, Technology and Innovation.

[39] S. Koemsoeun. 2020. Ministry changes its name, scope of operations. *The Phnom Penh Post*. 26 January. https://phnompenhpost.com/national/ministry-changes-its-name-scope-operations.

Assessment of Current Policy Approaches Related to 4IR

A diagnostic approach was taken to understand two important aspects of Cambodia's 4IR policy approach: (i) "the what"—the specific policies being adopted by Cambodia and how they compare to a set of best practice approaches seen internationally in preparing workers for 4IR; and (2) "the how"—the implementation mechanisms supporting 4IR efforts in government.

Assessment of Policy Actions ("The What")

The country's policies and programs have been grouped into nine action areas assessed to be most crucial to managing the impact of 4IR on jobs and skills.[40] Figure 41 shows the current degree of focus for each action area, rated as strong, moderate, or weak. This rating is based on scope and scale of each policy action vis-à-vis those observed in international best practices.

Overall, the current degree of focus on the range of 4IR-relevant policy areas is relatively low in Cambodia. A moderate level of focus has been placed on stimulating higher technology adoption by firms (largely through start-up creation efforts) and fostering government–industry–civil society collaboration on retraining frameworks. However, limited focus has been demonstrated in the areas of building awareness of in-demand jobs and skills, creating incentives for skills development, establishing lifelong learning models, ensuring the relevance and agility of education and training curricula to emerging skill needs, encouraging a focus on skills, building inclusive models for underserved groups, and creating social protection mechanisms for the emerging class of gig economy workers. More specifically:

(i) **Stimulating industry adoption and worker reskilling.** In the DII Global 4IR Readiness Index 2016, Cambodia was ranked 115th out of 120 countries assessed globally on their readiness for 4IR, behind neighboring ASEAN countries such as Viet Nam (91st), the Philippines (44th), and Indonesia (41st).[41] One particular challenge is around raising awareness of in demand skills. In-country consultations with stakeholders reveal a lack of national or industry-wide frameworks that map job opportunities and their associated skills to 4IR needs. A further challenge in this area relates to incentivizing employers and workers to engage in skill development. Currently, investment by employers in their workers' skills development is scant; the Employer Survey undertaken by the National Employment Agency in 2017 found that less than one-fifth (16%) of firms in Cambodia provided some form of training for their employees.[42] Employee training rates were also found to be low in the two focus industries: 10% in garment manufacturing, and for tourism, it ranged from 5% for food and beverage services companies to 19% accommodation services. In-country consultations revealed that due to insufficient employer-led training and given the large skills gap, industry associations are leading the way in undertaking worker training.[43] This is also consistent with the employer survey results in Chapter 2 that shows that only 10% of employers (in garment manufacturing) believe that graduates are

40   This is based on AlphaBeta research on international best practices for policy actions that manage the impact of Industry 4.0 on jobs and skills. Microsoft and AlphaBeta. 2019. *Preparing for AI: The Implications of Artificial Intelligence for Jobs and Skills in Asian Economies.* https://news.microsoft.com/apac/2019/08/26/preparing-for-ai-the-implications-of-artificial-intelligence-for-jobs-and-skills-in-asian-economies/.

41   These indices include the DII Global Industry 4.0 Readiness Index 2016, the World Economic Forum Networked Readiness Index 2016, and the Cornell INSEAD Global Innovation Index. Government of Cambodia, Ministry of Commerce. 2019. *Cambodia Trade Integration Strategy 2019-2023.* https://www.moc.gov.kh/Portals/0/Docs/OfficialDocs/CTIS-20190725143301726.pdf.

42   National Employment Agency. 2017. *Skills Shortages and Skills Gaps in the Cambodian Labour Market: Evidence from Employer Survey 2017.* http://www.nea.gov.kh/images/survay/ESNS%202017--Final--05282018.pdf.

43   This is based on consultations with the Cambodia Garment Training Institute and the Cambodian Federation of Employers and Business Associations in July 2019.

Figure 41: Degree of Focus of Policy Actions to Manage the Impact of 4IR on Jobs and Skills

Degree of current focus:[a] | ■ Strong ■ Moderate ■ Weak

Action Agenda	Key Action	Assessment
Stimulate 4IR adoption and worker reskilling efforts	Ensure strong and even adoption of 4I Racross firms and workers	■
	Build awareness of "in-demand" jobs and skills, as well as the benefits and opportunities of training	■
	Incentivize employers and workers to participate in skills development	■
	Foster close collaboration between governments, industry, and civil society to create relevant and effective nationwide retraining frameworks	■
Create new flexible qualification pathways	Establish effective lifelong learning models	■
	Ensure relevance and agility of education and training curriculums to emerging skill needs	■
	Encourage focus on skills rather than just qualifications in both recruitment and national labor market strategies	■
Build inclusiveness to extend 4IR benefits to all workers	Build inclusive models that allow underserved groups to benefit from 4IR	■
	Create social protection mechanisms for workers taking on flexible forms of labor	■

4IR = Industry 4.0 or Fourth Industrial Revolution.

[a] Degree of focus was assessed based on the following criteria: "Strong" –few or no gaps between the country's coverage of policy actions and coverage seen in international best practices; "Moderate" –medium level of gaps between the country's coverage of policy actions and coverage seen in international best practices; "Weak" –significant gaps between the country's coverage of policy actions and coverage seen in international best practices.

Source: Asian Development Bank and AlphaBeta.

well prepared for entry-level positions. On a more positive note, there has been significant effort to strengthen the adoption of 4IR technologies, and to foster closer collaboration between governments, industry, and civil society to create retraining frameworks.

(ii) **Creating new flexible qualification pathways.** With relatively low primary and secondary enrollment rates and no specific lifelong policies currently implemented, there is still some way to go to achieving lifelong learning in Cambodia—particularly in an era of rapidly changing technologies.[44] Education institutes in Cambodia are starting to include a focus on 4IR within their curricula. However, this is still limited in scale and largely applies only in leading institutions. In addition, the country still places strong emphasis on traditional qualifications attained through the education system or competency assessments—as opposed to previous work experience and skills gained.

---

[44] Cambodia experiences relatively low primary and secondary enrollment rates, with only 37% of those of eligible school age enrolled in secondary education—equivalent to less than half of the ASEAN median of 79% ASEAN Secretariat. 2018. *ASEAN Key Figures 2018*. https://www.aseanstats.org/wp-content/uploads/2018/12/ASEAN-Key-Figures-2018.pdf.

(iii) **Building inclusiveness to extend the benefits of 4IR to underserved communities.** While 4IR can help bring about greater productivity and wealth, it can also highlight existing vulnerabilities faced by certain segments of the labor market that do not have access to technology. This is a potentially great source of risk in Cambodia, where 77% of workers who live in rural areas are employed in "vulnerable jobs," which refer to work in precarious conditions (e.g., unsafe environments such as unregulated construction sites) and/or jobs with uncertain income flows (e.g., unpaid family workers).[45] Yet, there is limited evidence of strong government focus on building greater inclusiveness to allow underserved groups access to better opportunities in the labor market, let alone train them in preparation for 4IR—with most of such programs being undertaken by the private sector and nongovernment organizations.

Assessment of Implementation of 4IR Policies ("The How")

Implementation of Cambodia's 4IR strategy for jobs and skills was assessed against three dimensions found to be crucial for success according to past academic work: (i) clarity and robustness of plans, (ii) strength of coordination between different stakeholders, and (iii) alignment of financing and incentives (Figure 42).[46]

At this nascent stage, there is much room to strengthen Cambodia's implementation approach of its 4IR skills strategy. While the country has led with a relatively strong vision for its 4IR strategy, detailed implementation strategies have yet to be determined. There appears to be weak coordination across government departments on 4IR policy, and poor alignment between government, industry, and training and education institutes. Minimal government financing appears to have been deployed specifically for 4IR, and incentives for nongovernment stakeholders (employers and workers) to invest in skills development are limited. More specifically:

(i) **Clarity and robustness of plans.** For 4IR implementation be successful, a clear and robust strategy, with a strong understanding of what 4IR entails and the socioeconomic opportunities it poses, is crucial. While the country's 4IR strategy appears to be clear in both its vision and high-level strategies, and is forward-looking and premised on a local evidence base (e.g., the Cambodia Trade Integration Strategy conducts a thorough review of applicable 4IR technologies in the country's four major sectors: agriculture, garment manufacturing, tourism, and light manufacturing) (footnote 29), it is less clear about detailed implementation arrangements. Given the nascent stage of its 4IR policy, however, the degree of integration with the country's skills and education policies is relatively weak.

(ii) **Strength of coordination between different stakeholders.** For a clear and robust 4IR and skills policy to translate into positive implementation outcomes, there must be a strong level of coordination within and between the government, the education sector, industry, and training institutions. This appears to be weak in Cambodia's context, with poorly aligned 4IR understanding across ministries, limited coordination within the education sector on the TVET and academic streams, and weak communication between industry and training institutions on the skills demanded by industry.

---

45   ILO. 2015. *Rural development and employment opportunities in Cambodia; How can a national employment policy contribute toward realization of decent work in rural areas?* https://www.ilo.org/wcmsp5/groups/public/---asia/---ro-bangkok/documents/publication/wcms_228280.pdf.

46   Based on AlphaBeta research of Industry 4.0 strategies, plus insights from past public sector research, including: M. Barber. 2007. *Instruction to Deliver: Fighting to Transform Britain's Public Services*; and E. Daly and S. Singham. 2012. *Delivery 2.0: The New Challenge for Governments*. McKinsey & Company. https://www.mckinsey.com/industries/public-sector/our-insights/delivery-20-the-new-challenge-for-governments.

Figure 42: Implementation Challenges Associated with 4IR Policies for Jobs and Skills

Degree of current focus:[a] ■ Strong ■ Moderate ■ Weak

Dimension	Questions	Assessment
Clarity and robustness of plans	Is there a clearly articulated vision for 4IR?	Moderate
	Is there strong integration between employment and skills and the 4IR plan?	Weak
	Is the plan forward looking, incorporating 4IR trends?	Strong
	Is there strong local data to support evidence-based policymaking?	Strong
Strength of coordination	Is there one shared roadmap across industry and government departments for 4IR?	Moderate
	Is there coordination across different government ministries and levels?	Weak
	Is there strong alignment within and between industry, and education and training institutions?	Weak
Alignment of financing & incentives	Is the government financing aligned with the strategic goals?	Weak
	What are the strength of incentives for employers and workers to invest in skill development? What are the strength of incentives for teachers and institutions to ensure high-quality training and education systems?	Weak

[a] Degree of focus was assessed based on the following criteria: "Strong" –few or no gaps between the country's policy implementation approach and approach seen in international best practices; "Moderate" –medium level of gaps between the country's policy implementation approach and approach seen in international best practices; "Weak" –significant gaps between the country's policy implementation approach and approach seen in international best practices.

Source: Asian Development Bank and AlphaBeta.

(iii) **Alignment of financing and incentives.** For jobs and skills policies to be successful in mitigating the potential negative impacts of 4IR, funding and incentives would need to be well-aligned to ensure different stakeholders contribute to skills development. Government financing in Cambodia, while growing, does not appear to be sufficient to achieve the country's bold vision of leapfrogging from its current state of technology adoption (which has been characterized as being at the Industry 2.0 stage) to 4IR. At the same time, the incentives for employers, teachers, training institutes, and even students and their families to contribute toward skills development have been assessed to be weak.

CHAPTER 4

The Way Forward

The previous chapters highlighted a series of challenges facing Cambodia in relation to Industry 4.0 (4IR). This chapter summarizes those challenges and identifies several recommendations (based on relevant best practice in other countries) for how these could be addressed.

The COVID-19 Effect

The study was undertaken and completed prior to the spread of the coronavirus disease (COVID-19) that has caused unprecedented disruptions to labor markets and to the activities of the workforce across the world. This study's policy recommendations and strategies to strengthen widespread digital capabilities, enhance online/distant learning, digital platforms, education technology (or edtech), and simulation-based learning have become all the more relevant in the aftermath of COVID-19. The key approaches discussed and elaborated in the report bear great relevance to the current context of countries experiencing nationwide closures of schools and training institutes. The expectation is also that post-COVID-19, there would be operating procedures that constitute a new normal that entails far more digital capabilities in the workplace. Hence, the findings of this study and the follow-on policy directions are very timely and crucial for facilitating a sustainable bounce-back from COVID-19 strategy.

The two sectors chosen for the study in Cambodia, garment and tourism, have been adversely affected by the pandemic. Tourism worldwide practically ground to a halt due to COVID-19. The scale of cancellations and other disruptions required a greater use of digital tools and capabilities to the new normal. Meanwhile, workers in the garment manufacturing industry have suffered from massive layoffs as factories began closing down due to internal supply constraints and external demand shocks caused by COVID-19. Hence, the upskilling and reskilling on 4IR-related occupations is even more urgent for the revival of the economy and economic stimulus needed post-COVID-19.

The study does not address the implications of COVID-19 in Cambodia. However, the policy directions and future investments for higher-order skills, particularly in the digital domain, are eminently suitable for the country to reimagine new beginnings for the two sectors.

Recap of 4IR-Related Challenges Facing Cambodia

Figure 43 provides a recap of the challenges facing Cambodia from the industry analysis (Chapter 1), the training institute survey (Chapter 2), and the policy assessment (Chapter 3).

Figure 43: Recap of Challenges Facing Cambodia in Relation to 4IR

Area		Key Challenges	Factoids
Sector-level analysis	1	Large displacement of workers in certain sectors, with large gender implications	Up to 12% of jobs could be displaced by 4IR technologies in garment manufacturing
	2	Limited understanding of 4IR technologies by firms	Only 28% of garment manufacturing employers have a good understanding of 4IR technologies
	3	Large shift in tasks and skill requirements	4IR technologies could lead to >20% fall in worker time spent on routine physical tasks by 2030
	4	Significant ramp up of on-the-job training, particularly for analytical skills	Roughly 57%–77% of new trainings related to 4IR will need to be delivered on-the-job
Training institute survey	5	Lack of robust quality certification processes for courses	65% of all training institutions believe developing robust quality certification processes are important
	6	Limited adoption of 4IR technologies in the classroom	Only 8% of training institutions are using virtual learning platforms
	7	Mismatch on skill expectations	While 59% of training institutions believe graduates are well-prepared for entry-level positions, but only 10%–21% of employers
Policy assessment	8	Lack of flexible skill certification programs	Strong focus on traditional qualifications
	9	Lack of incentives for investment by firms in worker training	Most worker training being undertaken by industry associations rather than employers
	10	Lack of inclusive skilling opportunities and social protection mechanisms for flexible workers	Programs to build inclusiveness in the labor market, where they exist, lack scale
	11	Lack of integrated 4IR and skills policy, and coordination between government departments	Cambodia's 4IR strategy has a clearly articulated vision but limited integration with the country's skills strategy

Source: Asian Development Bank and AlphaBeta.

Recommendations to Address Challenges

There are a number of areas wherein Cambodia could strengthen its approach to 4IR. Drawing upon international and regional best practices related to the challenges highlighted above, several recommendations have been outlined to strengthen Cambodia's approach in terms of policy scope and implementation (Table 3). For each recommendation, a series of steps or possible approaches have been laid out as a practical road map for implementation in Cambodia. Table 2 shows the key entity suggested to take the lead for each recommendation, as well as the other stakeholders to be involved. These entities span across the government, industry, and education and training sectors, reflecting the importance of strong multi-stakeholder partnerships for implementing these recommendations.

Table 2: Suggested Leads and Stakeholders to Engage for Potential Actions in Recommendations to Strengthen 4IR Approach

No	Recommendation	Key Suggested Lead/s	Stakeholders to Involve
1	Develop Industry 4.0 (4IR) transformation road maps for key sectors	Joint committee constituting the Ministry of Economy and Finance (MEF) and the Ministry of Labor and Vocational Training (MLVT)	Industry associations and relevant sector training bodies (e.g., Cambodia Garment Training Institute) Key employers in each industry with experience in 4IR training for workers Training institutions Higher education institutions
2	Develop a series of industry-led TVET programs targeting skills for 4IR	Key employers in each industry	Industry associations and industry-wide training bodies Higher education institutions Training institutions National Training Board (under the MLVT) MEF
3	Strengthen quality assurance mechanisms for training institutions	National Training Board	Training institutions Industry associations and training bodies (including representatives from key companies with strong training programs in each sector)
4	Upgrade training delivery through 4IR technology in classrooms and training facilities	Ministry of Education, Youth and Sport	Ministry of Industry, Science, Technology and Innovation Education technology (edtech) companies
5	Develop flexible and modular skill certification programs	National Training Board	Industry associations (including representatives from key companies with strong training programs in each sector) Training institutions
6	Implement an incentive scheme for firms to train employees for 4IR	MEF	Industry associations (including representatives from key companies with strong training programs in each sector) Training institutions
7	Formulate new approaches and measures to strengthen inclusion and social protection in the context of 4IR	Ministry of Education, Youth and Sports and MLVT	Technology companies (to collaborate with the government to deliver digital skills training programs) Local authorities (to collaborate with the government to develop community learning centers) Universities (to collaborate with the government to create online courses in 4IR-related subjects for the public)

Source: Asian Development Bank and AlphaBeta.

Table 3: Examples of 4IR Skills-Related Best Practices from Around the World

There are a range of relevant best practices that could be adopted to tackle these challenges

No	Recommendation	Common Challenges	Examples of Countries where Recommendation was Implemented
1	Develop 4IR transformation road maps for key sectors	• Lack of understanding of 4IR by businesses • Large displacement of workers in certain sectors, with large gender implications • Lack of integrated 4IR and skills policy, and coordination between government departments	Australia, Singapore
2	Develop a series of industry-led TVET programs targeting skills for 4IR	• Significant ramp up of on-the-job training, particularly for analytical skills • Mismatch on skills expectations	Denmark, Finland, France, Germany, India, Norway, Switzerland
3	Strengthen quality assurance mechanisms for training institutions	• Lack of effective certification and quality assurance mechanisms in training	Australia, Ireland, Switzerland
4	Upgrade training delivery through 4IR technology in classrooms and training facilities	• Limited adoption of 4IR technologies in the classroom	South Africa
5	Develop flexible and modular skill certification programs	• Lack of flexible skill certification programs	Malaysia
6	Implement an incentive scheme for firms to train employees for 4IR	• Lack of incentives for investment by firms in worker training	Malaysia, Singapore
7	Formulate new approaches and measures to strengthen inclusion and social protection in the context of 4IR	• Lack of inclusive skilling opportunities and social protection mechanisms for vulnerable workers	Australia, Japan, Malaysia, Republic of Korea

4IR = Industry 4.0 or Fourth Industrial Revolution, TVET = technical and vocational education and training.

Source: Asian Development Bank and AlphaBeta.

Recommendation 1: Develop 4IR transformation road maps for key sectors.

While the Government of Cambodia has developed a broad strategy for leapfrogging from Industry 2.0 to 4IR, a key gap found in Chapter 3 was the lack of a well-integrated technology adoption and skills development strategy. How to ensure the development of both, in parallel, was also raised during an in-country workshop with government stakeholders.

A starting point to deepening coordination on 4IR skills development can be the development of sector-specific Industry Transformation Maps (ITMs) similar to Singapore, which provide information on technology impacts, career pathways, and the skills required for different occupations and reskilling options (Box 7).[47]

---

[47] SkillsFuture Singapore. 2019. Skills framework. https://www.skillsfuture.sg/skills-framework.

Box 7: Singapore Industry Transformation Maps

Singapore's Industry 4.0 (4IR) effort, comprising the Industry Transformation Maps (ITMs), is championed by a dedicated body, the Future Economy Council (FEC). Chaired by the Deputy Prime Minister, the FEC is represented by members from the government, industry, unions, and educational and training institutes.[a] Each ITM represents the road map to 4IR technology adoption for an industry.[b] To ensure coordination and accountability within the government, each ITM is championed by a different government agency whose purview is most relevant to the industry. For example, the ITM for the manufacturing sector is led by the Economic Development Agency, while that for the built environment sector is led by the Building and Construction Authority.

The Skills Framework is a key component of the ITMs. Co-created by industry, government, and civil society stakeholders, the framework provides key information on career pathways, existing and emerging skills required for different occupations, and reskilling options for different industries. It also provides a list of training programs for skills upgrading. By virtue of its multi-stakeholder nature, this framework is also intended to benefit not just workers, but also employers (in enabling them to identify emerging skill needs for their workers and enhance talent attraction and retention efforts), training providers (in allowing them to gain better insights into emerging skill trains and more optimally target critical skill gaps through appropriate courses), and students (in facilitating them to make informed decisions on choice of study based on career aspirations). A 2018 survey of over 700 firms in Singapore found that 36% of firms take guidance from the ITMs on how to improve their talent pipeline, and how they could address manpower challenges for different sectors.

[a] Government of Singapore, Ministry of Trade and Industry. 2020. The Future Economy Council. https://www.mti.gov.sg/FutureEconomy/TheFutureEconomyCouncil; Government of Singapore, Ministry of Education. 2016. *Formation of the Council for Skills, Innovation and Productivity*. https://www.moe.gov.sg/news/press-releases/formation-of-the-council-for-skills--innovation-and-productivity.
[b] Government of Singapore, Ministry of Trade and Industry. 2017. *Media factsheet- Industry Transformation Maps*. https://www.mti.gov.sg/-/media/MTI/ITM/General/Fact-sheet-on-Industry-Transformation-Maps---revised-as-of-31-Mar-17.pdf.

Source: S. K. Tang. 2019. Singapore Businesses Not Investing Enough In Employee Training: SBF Survey. *Channel News Asia*. https://www.channelnewsasia.com/news/business/singapore-companies-not-investing-employee-training-sbf-survey-11134230.

In Cambodia, the development of these road maps could be led by a joint committee formed by the Ministry of Economy and Finance (MEF) (due to the link between 4IR adoption and economic development) and the Ministry of Labor and Vocational Training (MLVT) (due to the focus on workforce skills development). These road maps should also be coordinated with or serve as an extension of the country's recently developed "sector skill councils" that comprise industry associations and training institutes.[48] Taking reference from the ITMs, a stronger complementary focus on the relevant 4IR technologies for each industry could inform the skill requirements by industry that will be critical to ensuring 4IR readiness for workers. These road maps could be developed for Cambodia's garment manufacturing and tourism industries. In garment manufacturing, focus should be placed on building upon the competency standards that have already been developed by the Cambodia Garment Training Institute (CGTI), which was formed in 2017 to address critical skill shortages through undertaking worker training for the industry. In developing these road maps, the MEF and MLVT should work closely with

48   Consultation with the MLVT in July 2019; ADB. 2018. Toward Adopting a Skills Development Fund for Cambodia. *ADB Briefs* No. 90. February. https://www.adb.org/sites/default/files/publication/401746/adb-brief-090-skills-development-fund-cambodia.pdf.

Box 8: Connecting Students and Industry with Boot Camps

Industry needs appropriately trained recruits, and youth job seekers need to be hired. Industry boot camps can help connect the skills offered by young job seekers to those needed by industry. The "Generation Program" develops programs focusing on four sectors with teaching facilities in 119 cities in six continents. The program is offered to 18- to 29-year-olds.[a] Its features include direct contact with potential employers; matching trainee attributes with employer needs; courses that cover technical, behavioral, and mental skills; continuous monitoring and support during and after the program; and a strong alumni network.

Since its inception, 31,600 people have gone through the training with 80% finding jobs within 3 months of finishing the program, and 65% of those stayed with their jobs for at least 1 year. Employers also rate program graduates as higher performing than their peers.[b]

[a] Generation Program. https://www.generation.org/.
[b] Asia Philanthropy Circle. 2017. *Catalysing Productive Livelihood: A Guide to Education Interventions with an Accelerated Path to Scale and Impact.* http://www.edumap-indonesia.asiaphilanthropycircle.org/wp-content/uploads/2017/11/APC-Giving-Guide-Book-Final-Report-17112017.pdf.

Source: Asian Development Bank and AlphaBeta.

industry bodies such as CGTI, employers with deep experience in training workers on 4IR skills, as well as training and higher education institutions in the country.

Recommendation 2: Develop a series of industry-led TVET programs targeting skills for 4IR.

A major stumbling block in Cambodia's skills readiness for 4IR is the poor quality of technical and vocational education and training (TVET) programs. In particular, the lack of industry relevance of such programs was flagged as a key gap in Chapter 3. To strengthen the quality and relevance of TVET programs, it is recommended that the government work with employers to develop industry-led TVET programs. Such programs not only help to reduce the government's fiscal burden, but also provide employers a ready pool of trained talent for recruitment. Some notable examples of such programs abroad include industry boot camps by McKinsey & Company's Generation program, which operates across several countries (Box 8).[49]

Industry-led TVET programs could be led by key employers in each industry. Employers can work together with industry associations, as well as training and education institutions to scope the programs and recruit trainers, with support from the labor or manpower ministries. Parameters to be designed include training curricula (including which 4IR technologies can be taught) and their durations, teacher recruitment and training, and applicant criteria. In defining the parameters of such programs, the formats observed in international best practices may be considered. The MEF's Skills Development Fund pilot could be a potential source of financing mechanism for these collaborations, while the National Training Board under the MLVT could offer support in the form of institutionalizing formal course accreditations for such programs.

---

[49] Asia Philanthropy Circle. 2017. *Catalysing productive livelihood: A Guide to Education Interventions with an Accelerated Path to Scale and Impact.* http://www.edumap-indonesia.asiaphilanthropycircle.org/wp-content/uploads/2017/11/APC-Giving-Guide-Book-Final-Report-17112017.pdf.

Such programs should build upon existing industry efforts to train workers. For instance, garment manufacturing companies could work with the CGTI to ensure that they do not duplicate the efforts of the institute, but instead fill in the gaps of high-demand skills for which training programs do not currently exist. The companies behind future industry-led TVET programs could also leverage the CGTI's network to publicize their programs; the CGTI regularly organizes TVET awareness campaigns in high schools across different provinces to educate students on the TVET system and job opportunities that come with it.[50]

Recommendation 3: Strengthen quality assurance mechanisms for training institutions.

In the survey of training institutions (Chapter 2), 65% of respondents highlighted quality assurance mechanisms as the most impactful area for policy intervention. Governments in countries across the world are also increasingly requiring evidence that there is a labor market need for new programs. This is the case for TVET programs in Australia, France, Hungary, Ireland, Poland, the Republic of Korea, Sweden, and the United States (US). Such labor market needs can be demonstrated in a variety of ways: for example, surveys of demand (Austria), employers' opinions (Denmark and Lithuania), agreements with employers to provide traineeship places (Hungary), and evidence of alignment with skills gap (Ireland).[51] While establishing institution–industry partnerships highlighted earlier may help address some of the quality assurance concerns, it will also be important to understand the 4IR readiness of the quality assurance mechanisms in place in Cambodia, and to consider mechanisms to strengthen these approaches.

This initiative can be led by the National Training Board under the MLVT, which oversees training accreditations in the country. The quality assurance mechanisms can be scoped in tandem with training institutions, and it should take into consideration feedback from industries (given their experience in recruiting graduates from the programs) on the parameters to consider when assessing the quality of various programs.

Recommendation 4: Upgrade training delivery through 4IR technology in classrooms and training facilities.

An effective way of preparing students or future workers for 4IR—or at least equipping them with the basic computer literacy skills necessary to excel in the future economy—is to apply 4IR technologies in classrooms. Representatives from TVET institutions and employers have also cited a lack of basic technical knowledge due to gaps in basic education as a major issue impacting TVET outcomes.[52]

Artificial intelligence (AI) technology, for example, has been used to stimulate critical thinking through applying a virtual environment for building and assessing higher order inquiry skills.[53] AI-enabled immersive computer games, for instance, has been used for science, technology, engineering, and mathematics or STEM education in some schools in the US.[54] Personalized learning approaches adopting digital channels in which students access customized learning content through online

---

[50]   This is based on consultation with the CGTI in July 2019.

[51]   ILO. 2020. Skills for Employment: Global Public–Private Knowledge Sharing Platform. https://www.skillsforemployment.org/KSP/en/index.htm

[52]   This is based on the country workshop conducted in October 2019.

[53]   J. Spector and S. Ma. 2019. Inquiry and critical thinking skills for the next generation: from artificial intelligence back to human intelligence. *Smart Learning Environments*. 11 September. https://slejournal.springeropen.com/articles/10.1186/s40561-019-0088-z.

[54]   D. Ketelhut et al. 2009. A multi-user virtual environment for building and assessing higher order inquiry skills in science. *British Journal of Educational Technology*. 20 December. https://onlinelibrary.wiley.com/doi/abs/10.1111/j.1467-8535.2009.01036.x.

Box 9: Leveraging Technologies to Improve Education and Manage Gender Gaps

Digital technologies have been shown to improve education quality and even manage gender gaps starting from an early age.

The African School for Excellence (ASE), an affordable private secondary school in South Africa, deploys an innovative rotational classroom model in which students rotate between teacher-facilitated lessons, small-group peer-learning activities, and individual work on computers supervised by trainee teachers. Deploying online courses from free products such as Khan Academy, this blended learning approach innovatively reduces costs through its reliance on a smaller number of highly trained teachers, while enhancing education outcomes with its emphasis on personalized learning and small class sizes. ASE students have been found to outperform the wealthiest students in the country by 2.3 times in mathematics and 1.4 times in English.[a] At the same time, the per student cost of $800 a year is low when compared with South African averages that range from $1,400 to $16,500 per year.

Such personalized adaptive learning digital tools are also beginning to show their potential in bridging gender differences in students' attainment from a young age. "onebillion," a London-based nonprofit organization focused on building scalable educational software for children, launched the application "onecourse," which delivers content and practice on a tablet.[b] This application was found to prevent a gender gap in reading and mathematics skills from surfacing among first-grade students in Malawi—potentially by overcoming sociocultural factors responsible for gaps emerging in traditional classroom settings.[c]

[a] D. Istance and A. Paniagua. 2019. *Learning to Leapfrog: Innovative Pedagogies to Transform Education*. Center for Universal Education at Brookings Institution. https://www.brookings.edu/wp-content/uploads/2019/09/Learning-to-Leapfrog-InnovativePedagogiestoTransformEducation-Web.pdf.
[b] onebillion. onecourse: one app that delivers reading, writing and numeracy. https://onebillion.org/onecourse/app/.
[c] Pathways for Prosperity Commission. 2019. *Positive Disruption: Health and Education in the Digital Age*. https://pathwayscommission.bsg.ox.ac.uk/positive-disruption.

Source: Asian Development Bank and AlphaBeta.

---

education programs could also be incorporated into formal curricula. However, as shown in the training institution survey results, technology adoption in the classroom in Cambodia is currently limited in many institutions (particularly related to technologies such as virtual learning platforms).

This is an area in which the Ministry of Education, Youth, and Sport (MOEYS) could spearhead, and work with the recently established Ministry of Industry, Science, Technology and Innovation as well as education technology (or edtech) firms to incorporate 4IR technologies in classrooms from elementary schools all the way through to universities, polytechnics, and TVET institutions. A possible way to reduce the overall fiscal burden is to adopt blended learning approaches as installing such technologies and equipment at every institution could be fiscally challenging. Such approaches combine both classroom and personalized online learning and have been demonstrated to be highly effective at not just improving education outcomes, but also managing gender inequality (Box 9). Further, 4IR technologies that are already adopted in garment manufacturing and tourism can also be taught directly in classroom environments. For instance, students can be familiarized with smartphone applications and their development (which are increasingly used in the tourism industry) as well as automation, 3D printing, and graphic design software (4IR technologies for the garment manufacturing industry, some of which have already been deployed).

Box 10: The Malaysian Skills Certification Program

In Malaysia, individuals who do not possess formal educational qualifications have the opportunity to enter into their desired careers through the Malaysian Skills Certification Program.

Recognized by industry, this program awards Skills Certificates at five different levels:[a]

   (i)   Malaysian Skills Certificate (SKM) Level 1
   (ii)   Malaysian Skills Certificate (SKM) Level 2
   (iii)   Malaysian Skills Certificate (SKM) Level 3
   (iv)   Diploma in Skills Malaysia (DKM) Level 4
   (v)   Malaysian Skills Advanced Diploma (DLKM) Level 5

These certificates are awarded across all sectors of the economy—classified into 22 sectors —according to the country's National Occupational Skills Standard.[b] Importantly, no former educational qualifications are required—the only requirements for candidates are the ability to speak and write in both Bahasa Melayu and English, and the need to have passed a lower Skills Certificate level before being able to qualify for a higher level in the same field.

Candidates may obtain these certificates through three channels: training in institutions accredited by the *Jabatan Pembangunan Kemahiran* (Department of Skills Development), industry apprenticeships under the National Dual Training System, and through sufficient Accreditation of Prior Achievement. The third channel refers to accreditation gained through evidence of past work and/or training experience.

With these certificates being accredited as officially recognized qualifications and mapped to equivalent academic qualifications under the Malaysian Qualifications Framework, Malaysian companies are able to take guidance from this framework when assessing the suitability of job candidates without formal education, but who possess the relevant skills to excel at the job.[c]

[a] Government of Malaysia, Department of Skills Development. Malaysian Skill Certificate (SKM). https://www.dsd.gov.my/index.php/en/service/malaysian-skills-certificate.
[b] OECD. 2012. *Skills Development Pathways in Asia.* https://www.oecd.org/cfe/leed/Skills%20Development%20Pathways%20in%20Asia_FINAL%20VERSION.pdf.
[c] Government of Malaysia, Ministry of Higher Education and Malaysian Qualifications Agency. 2011. *Malaysian Qualifications Framework.* http://www2.mqa.gov.my.

Source: Asian Development Bank and AlphaBeta.

Recommendation 5: Develop flexible and modular skill certification programs.

As outlined in Chapter 3, there is still a strong emphasis on traditional qualifications attained through the education system or competency assessments. This recommendation thus encourages a stronger focus on skills—beyond such traditional qualifications—including in both the garment manufacturing and tourism industries. This would involve (i) reviewing the need for minimum educational qualifications and competency-based assessments in current certification frameworks (together with industry and training institutions); (ii) analyzing the potential impact of replacing such criteria with evidence of skills attainment from pathways such as accredited training programs, industry apprenticeships, and certificates recognizing learning through past work experience (potentially taking reference from Malaysia's Skills Certification Framework, Box 10); and (iii) synchronizing these processes with the conventional certifications based on academic qualifications (ensuring they are recognized by employers).

Such programs could be led by the National Training Board and build on current existing efforts by industry associations and training institutions. For example, the CGTI has already developed a set of competency standards and training programs for industry workers.[55] With over 600 company members that contribute a mandatory training levy of $1 per worker per year, this program is relatively well supported by employers and can be a starting point for developing flexible skill certification programs specific to the industry.

Recommendation 6: Implement an incentive scheme for firms to train employees for 4IR.

Despite the substantial productivity gains 4IR technologies can bring about (as demonstrated in Chapter 1), employer-led training efforts in Cambodia remain limited. The National Employment Agency's Employer Survey undertaken in 2017 found that less than one-fifth (16%) of firms in the country provided some form of training for their employees (footnote 42). Employee training rates were also found to be low in the two focus industries: 10% in the garment manufacturing industry, and within the tourism industry, this ranged from 5% for food and beverage services companies to 19% for hotels. The low training rate could be due to three factors:

(i)   There are information asymmetries pertaining to a limited awareness of the new skills that are required for 4IR. In-country consultations with stakeholders reveal a lack of national or industry-wide frameworks that map 4IR technologies to new skill needs.

(ii)   There appears to be a lack of well-functioning markets for training services in Cambodia, characterized by a shortage of high-quality training courses and instructors as well as information asymmetries about available training options. According to the 2017 Employer Survey conducted by the National Employment Agency, the largest barrier faced by employers in implementing formal workplace training was the lack of trainers and courses available (as cited by 36% of surveyed employers). Other key barriers cited were the low quality of courses available (27%) and the lack of information on courses and trainers (20%).

(iii) While employers in Cambodia are cognizant of the need to develop training plans for their employees, many lack the financial budgets to implement them. The 2017 Employer Survey reflected that although 72% of the firms surveyed had developed training plans, three-quarters of these firms were unable to allocate budgets to these plans. This finding was corroborated by stakeholder consultations undertaken with industry associations.

Given these factors, it is critical to develop a set of support programs to encourage firms to invest in relevant 4IR training for their workers. This will involve developing appropriate incentive programs for firms to invest in worker skill development related to 4IR. The MEF, in consultation with industry associations (including representatives from key companies with strong training programs in each sector) and training institutions, can lead the development of support programs, which can be done in four steps:

(i)   Identify appropriate incentive programs for firms (Box 11 provides some international examples).

(ii)   Undertake a holistic cost–benefit analysis of the incentive scheme and associated training programs (noting that cost–benefit analyses of skills training programs done from the government's perspective have tended to focus largely on the direct economic costs of the program, while disregarding indirect economic benefits such as reduced welfare payments due to lower unemployment rates resulting from the training).

---

[55]   This is based on consultation with the CGTI in July 2019.

Box 11: Incentive Schemes for Employee Training in the Region

The Government of Singapore provides subsidies for employee training course fees and absentee payroll salary costs, with higher incentives being awarded for courses that are government-certified.[a] For example, while subsidies for both government-certified and approved certifiable courses cover 90%–95% of course fees, those for the approved certifiable courses have hourly caps. On the other hand, the subsidies for non-certifiable courses are lower at S$2 per hour (equivalent to $1.44 per hour) of training. Absentee payroll funding is also accessible and covers up to 95% of hourly basic salary. The Government of Malaysia has a similar program called Skills Upgrading Program, which provides grants covering 70% of training fees for small and medium-sized enterprises or small and medium-sized enterprises for technical and soft skills.[b]

[a] SkillsFuture Singapore. Funding Support for Employers. https://www.ssg.gov.sg/programmes-and-initiatives/funding/funding-for-employer-based-training.html.
[b] SME Corp Malaysia. 2019. Skills upgrading programme. https://www.smecorp.gov.my/index.php/en/.

Source: Asian Development Bank and AlphaBeta.

(iii) Pilot programs in a number of priority industries (particularly in garment manufacturing and tourism).

(iv) Scale the program to other industries, incorporating lessons learned from the pilot. The ongoing Skills Development Fund pilot could be an appropriate platform to lead this work.[56]

Recommendation 7: Formulate new approaches and measures to strengthen inclusion and social protection in the context of 4IR.

With a substantial portion of the population belonging to low-income families and rural areas with few job opportunities as highlighted in Chapter 3, lifelong learning programs promoting inclusiveness in skills development in Cambodia is critical to ensure that the country's journey toward 4IR does not leave many behind. In developing targeted interventions, it is recommended that policy makers undertake an analysis to identify key vulnerable communities facing largest potential impact from 4IR, and work with relevant community leaders to scope targeted interventions. This is particularly important for the garment manufacturing and tourism industries, where the analysis in Chapter 1 found that 4IR is likely to impact women. Possible approaches include:

(i) **Working with education institutions and the private sector to develop 4IR courses for individuals at all levels of 4IR understanding**. The MOEYS and the MLVT could work together with universities and polytechnics to develop courses for the public that build citizens' awareness of 4IR. This has been implemented in both Japan and the Republic of Korea, where universities and polytechnics are encouraged by the government to develop localized learning programs open to all citizens age 25 years old and above.[57] The Government of Singapore worked with the private sector to develop a 3-hour "AI for Everyone" course to introduce people

---

[56] ADB. 2018. Toward Adopting a Skills Development Fund for Cambodia. *ADB Briefs* No. 90. February. https://www.adb.org/sites/default/files/publication/401746/adb-brief-090-skills-development-fund-cambodia.pdf.
[57] UNESCO Institute for Lifelong Learning. Republic of Korea: The 3rd National Lifelong Learning Promotion Plan: 2017, issued in 2013. http://uil.unesco.org/document/republic-korea-3rd-national-lifelong-learning-promotion-plan-2017-issued-2013; and UNESCO Institute for Lifelong Learning. Japan: Basic Plan for the Promotion of Education, issued in 2008. http://uil.unesco.org/document/japan-basic-plan-promotion-education-issued-2008.

to modern AI technologies and applications in everyday life.[58] In another example, Microsoft is establishing an AI school in India that will educate students on AI technologies across the age and experience spectrum. This aims to place young learners in good stead for future job opportunities, while also facilitating successful career transitions for adults of working age.[59] The MOEYS and the MLVT can consider similar collaborations with technology companies on such programs targeted at working professionals. There can also be opportunity to build on current programs such as the New Generation Schools where AI/computer programming and STEM are being promoted. There can be further opportunity to scale up the ongoing Skills Bridging Program, Voucher Skills Training Programs, and Basic Education Equivalency Program (BEEP), which have been piloted in past projects with the Asian Development Bank and the UN Educational, Scientific and Cultural Organization (UNESCO).[60]

(ii) **Developing a local network of community learning centers where such courses could take place.** The MLVT can work together with community leaders to identify or develop venues for learning. In the Republic of Korea, the government placed heavy emphasis on establishing an even distribution of lifelong learning centers in villages and provinces. In Viet Nam, one of the strategies in the government's Framework on Building a Learning Society in the Period of 2012–2020 is to increase the number of community learning centers and district-level continuing education centers.[61] Over 70 of such centers have been established across Viet Nam to offer alternative education support to individuals who were not able to access basic education opportunities, and about 10% of Viet Nam's workforce currently participate in such centers.[62] Besides these centers, workshops are also organized in museums and other cultural centers.[63] To promote learning beyond the formal education and training sectors, the Government of Japan utilizes local libraries and museums to deliver cultural learning programs for both children and adults.[64]

(iii) **Provide access to online learning channels.** This can be an effective intervention if physical access to educational or training institutions is a challenge, particularly for rural communities in Cambodia. For example, the Ministry of Higher Education in Malaysia encourages and supports universities to create massive open online courses (or MOOCs) in different subjects, which are mandated to be made available to the general public regardless of educational background, financial status, or geographical location (footnote 62). This mode of developing and promoting online distance learning courses through universities is also an important prong of Viet Nam's national lifelong learning strategy (footnote 63).

Industry-Specific Priorities

While these recommendations apply to both garment manufacturing and tourism, there is a set of priorities unique to each industry that should be considered when implementing the industry-specific policy actions. These priorities were formed based on the findings in the earlier chapters, as well as through in-country consultations with government, industry, and training and education sector stakeholders, and aim to tackle the underlying weaknesses in each industry's ability to reap the benefits from 4IR technologies.

[58] AI Singapore. AI for Everyone. https://www.aisingapore.org/talentdevelopment/ai4e/.

[59] Information shared by Microsoft on the company's Digital Skills program.

[60] Further details are available at Technical Vocational Education and Training Sector Development Program. http://tvetsdp.ntb.gov.kh/project-description-2/.

[61] UNESCO Institute for Lifelong Learning. Republic of Korea: The 3rd National Lifelong Learning Promotion Plan: 2017, issued in 2013. http://uil.unesco.org/document/republic-korea-3rd-national-lifelong-learning-promotion-plan-2017-issued-2013.

[62] UNESDOC Digital Library. 2017. *Lifelong learning in transformation: promising practices in Southeast Asia.* https://unesdoc.unesco.org/ark:/48223/pf0000253603.

[63] UNESCO Institute for Lifelong Learning. Vietnam: Framework on Building a learning society in the period 2012-2020, issued in 2013. http://uil.unesco.org/document/vietnam-framework-building-learning-society-period-2012-2020-issued-2013.

[64] UNESCO Institute for Lifelong Learning. Japan: Basic Plan for the Promotion of Education, issued in 2008. http://uil.unesco.org/document/japan-basic-plan-promotion-education-issued-2008.

Garment Manufacturing Industry

- **Address the potentially disproportionate impact of technological disruption on females.**
  Both the employer survey, and in-country consultations with industry representatives, government officials, and nongovernment organizations, revealed that females are likely to be disproportionately impacted by potential 4IR-related job displacement effects, given that they constitute a larger share of workers in the industry. It is thus important that the training programs described in the recommendations on incorporate gender-sensitive approaches (e.g., Recommendation 2 on industry-led TVET programs, Recommendation 5 on flexible skill certification programs, and Recommendation 7 on formulation of new training approaches for vulnerable workers). These programs can consider teaching pedagogies that have been demonstrated to be more effective for female learners (e.g., having female STEM role models as trainers).[65]

- **Enhance government and industry knowledge of 4IR technologies and their benefits.**
  The employer survey in Chapter 1 showed that the majority of garment manufacturing firms are unaware of the different types of and potential productivity benefits of 4IR technologies. Consultations with government stakeholders similarly revealed a limited understanding in these aspects—despite having broader awareness that 4IR is an important topic to address. This requires a strong focus on enhancing both government and industry stakeholders' understanding of 4IR in the early stage of any of the recommended policy actions. For example, before developing the skills framework within the sector-specific 4IR transformation road maps (Recommendation 1), government and industry stakeholders will have to work with technology firms and align on the types of 4IR technologies applicable to the industry. For the garment manufacturing industry, this list has been shared in Chapter 1.3.1. It would also be similarly important to cultivate this understanding in downstream employee training programs.

- **Support 4IR knowledge transfer from larger factories to smaller factories.** Cambodia's garment manufacturing industry is an ecosystem consisting of large, export-oriented factories contracted by major multinational apparel brands (e.g., Adidas, Gap, H&M) and a number of smaller factories that often act as subcontractors to the large factories. Being more well resourced and with stronger international networks, these large companies are generally in a more advanced stage of 4IR adoption and training than smaller factories. Due to high-quality industrial cutting and sewing requirements, global apparel brands have, in fact, introduced these currently implemented 4IR technologies in in Cambodia (footnote 29). On the other hand, smaller factories tend to be less exposed to new technologies, and, even if they are willing to, have limited financial and technical capacity to adopt them. There is thus a compelling push for knowledge transfer on 4IR adoption and skills development strategies from these larger factories to their smaller counterparts.
  The owners of these larger factories can also be instrumental to supporting many of the policy recommendations outlined—from formulating the 4IR transformation road maps for the garment manufacturing industry (Recommendation 1) to co-creating the skill certification programs (Recommendation 5) that the small factories can adopt and incorporate into their own training programs. Where the required competencies overlap, there could even be scope for consolidated training programs led by these large companies for the benefit of micro, small, and medium-sized enterprises (or MSMEs).

65   Microsoft. 2018. *Closing the STEM Gap: Why STEM Classes and Careers Still Lack Girls and What We Can Do About It.* https://query. prod.cms.rt.microsoft.com/cms/api/am/binary/RE1UMWz.

Tourism Industry

- **Leverage growth of domestic smartphone application development industry to build 4IR readiness.** The employer survey revealed that employers in the tourism sector currently have low levels of understanding of 4IR technologies (Chapter 2). In-country consultations with industry representatives, however, reveal an emerging domestic smartphone application development industry. Local developers have been responsible for a number of locally successful smartphone applications that are being used to book hotels, tours, and other tourism services (e.g., the Angkor Audio app provides audio-visual guides of Angkor Wat). Thus there is a strong potential for the tourism industry to leverage on the growth of local application developers to improve 4IR readiness. Hotels and food and beverage services companies can partner with local developers in creating applications that promote (e.g., in-app customer service reviews) and even broaden their services (e.g., app-enabled hotel concierges). Such partnerships could be instrumental to enhancing the effectiveness of the recommended actions, for example, in developing 4IR skills road maps (Recommendation 1) and industry-led training efforts (Recommendation 2).

- **Ensure focus on training communication and social skills.** The analysis in Chapter 1 reflected that as opposed to the garment manufacturing industry, 4IR-related disruptions in the tourism industry are likely to boost the importance of socio-emotional and interpersonal skills. As technological innovations help displace more routine and mundane tasks, more time will potentially be freed up for workers to focus on the more value-adding aspects of service delivery—personalized customer interactions. It is thus critical to ensure that all training programs delivered as part of the recommended actions include a focus on training for such skills.

- **Foster stronger coordination between training institutions and employers.** In-country consultations with employers in the industry revealed a strong mismatch between the type of training delivered and employers' skill requirements. In particular, stakeholders shared that most of the training options for the tourism industry (especially for food and beverage services) were for short-term courses that aim to address skills mismatches; however, such courses often yielded workers that were still unprepared for dealing with the actual job demands. With the added complexity that 4IR technologies would bring, stakeholders emphasized the importance of ensuring that sufficient funds and resources were invested in longer-term courses (some suggested at least 2-year courses) that help build foundational skill sets. This will be an important consideration for the recommendations that specify training programs for workers (e.g., Recommendation 2 on industry-led training programs and Recommendation 7 on new approaches for training vulnerable workers), as well as the recommendations for strengthening quality assurance mechanisms for training institutions (Recommendation 3) and on skill certification programs (Recommendation 4).

Participants Engaged During National Consultations

Together with the Asian Development Bank, the AlphaBeta team consulted government and industry stakeholders in a series of initial consultations in July 2019, and subsequently through a workshop in October 2019. Tables A1 and A2 list down the stakeholders consulted in both engagements.

Table A1: List of Stakeholders Engaged in Initial Consultations, July 2019

Entity	Stakeholders Engaged
Government Agencies	
Ministry of Labor and Vocational Training	• Pich Sophoan – Permanent Secretary of State • Hong Choeun – Secretary of State
Ministry of Economy and Finance	• Hem Vanndy – Under Secretary of State • Chhuon Samrith – Deputy Director-General
Directorate General of Technical Vocational Education and Training	• Hing Sideth – Director General • Thorng Samon – Deputy Director General
Ministry of Education, Youth and Sport	• Mak Ngoy – Director General for Higher Education • Put Samith – Director General For Education
Council for the Development of Cambodia	• Suon Sophal – Director of Public Relations and Promotions
Ministry of Industry, Science, Technology and Innovation (formerly known as Ministry of Industry and Handicrafts)	• Some Nara – Under Secretary of State • Sarik Phalla – Director, General Department of Industry, Department of Industrial Affairs
National Institute of Post, Telecoms and ICT	• Seng Sopheap – President
Training Institutes	
National Polytechnic Institute of Cambodia	• Seng Sokheng – Vice-President
Institute Technology of Cambodia	• Om Romny – Director General
Step IT Academy	• Rodionovs Vladimirs – Partner
Cambodia Garment Training Institute	• Andrew Tey – Center Director
Industry Associations	
Cambodian Federation of Employers and Business Associations	• Sopheab – Secretary-General • Sar Kinal – Treasurer
Others (Research institutes, multilateral organizations)	
Japan International Cooperation Agency, United Nations Industrial Development Organization, World Bank, Cambodia Development Resource Institute, International Labour Organization	

Source: Asian Development Bank and AlphaBeta.

Table A2: List of Stakeholders Engaged In Country Workshop, October 2019

Entity	Stakeholders Engaged
Government Agencies	
Ministry of Economy and Finance	• Phan Phalla, Under Secretary of State • Ung Luyna – Deputy Secretary General • Ky Sokkim – Deputy Director, Macroeconomic Policy Department • Hy Thy – M&E Specialist, Macroeconomic Policy Department • Chhoeung Norin My – Economist, Macroeconomic Policy Department • Chan Sephanron
Ministry of Post and Telecommunication	• Sok Puthyvuth – Secretary of State
Ministry of Labour and Vocational Training	• Hong Choeun – Secretary of State • Chan Phealadey – Deputy Director General, TVET
Ministry of Commerce	• Penn Sovicheat – Director General
Ministry of Planning, National Institute of Statistics	• Nor Vannd – Director, Department of Economic Statistics
Ministry of Education, Youth and Sport	• Lim Sothea – Director General • Sopheak Rey – Deputy Director General, Higher Education
Council for the Development of Cambodia	• Nut Unvoanra – Deputy Secretary General • Seng Sunly – Official Private Investment Strategy • Chea Kesorphearom – Official Private Investment Strategy
Industry	
Cambodian Federation of Employers and Business Associations	• Sar Kinal – Board Member • Yoeurm Boran – Research and Policy Manager
Cambodia Association of Travel Agents	• Meng Phala – Vice President
Cambodia Tourism Federation	• Channoline Nak – Manager
Education and Training Institutes	
National Polytechnic Institute of Cambodia	• Bun Phearin, Director • Seng Sokheng • Srang Sophea
Institute of Technology of Cambodia	• Om Romny – Director General
Pour Soir Enfants	• Emilie Deschaseaux – Dean
Academy of Culinary Arts Cambodia	• Pierre Tami – Director
Step IT Academy	• Nataly Rodionova – Managing Director

continued on next page

Table A2 *continued*

Entity	Stakeholders Engaged
Research Institutes	
Cambodia Research Development Institute	• Vathana Roth – Research Fellow
Multilateral Organizations	
Swedish International Development Cooperation Agency	• Magnus Saemundsson – Education Advisor
International Labour Organization	• Khleang Rim – Program Officer
United Nations Industrial Development Organization	• Sin Kang – Program Officer
Agence Française de Développement	• Chan Sorya – Program Officer
United Nations Development Program	• Vivak Nvon – Project Manager

Source: Asian Development Bank and AlphaBeta.

Bibliography

ACT/EMP and International Labour Organization (ILO). 2017. *ASEAN in Transformation: How Technology is Changing Jobs and Enterprises – Cambodia Country Brief*. https://www.ilo.org/actemp/publications/WCMS_579672/lang--en/index.htm.

Asian Development Bank (ADB). 2015. *Cambodia: Addressing the Skills Gap*. https://www.adb.org/sites/default/files/publication/176283/cambodia-addressing-skills-gap.pdf.

ADB. 2018. *Asian Development Outlook 2018 - How Technology Affects Jobs*. https://www.adb.org/publications/asian-development-outlook-2018-how-technology-affects-jobs.

———. 2018. *Cambodia's new Technical and Vocational Education and Training Policy*. https://www.adb.org/sites/default/files/publication/401691/adb-brief-089-cambodia-new-tvet-policy.pdf.

———. 2018. *Social Protection Brief: Reducing Youth Not in Employment, Education or Training through JobStart Philippines*. https://www.adb.org/sites/default/files/publication/396081/adb-brief-084-youth-not-employment.pdf.

_____. 2018. Toward Adopting a Skills Development Fund for Cambodia. *ADB Briefs* No. 90. February. https://www.adb.org/sites/default/files/publication/401746/adb-brief-090-skills-development-fund-cambodia.pdf.

ADB–BAPPENAS. 2019. *Policies to Support the Development of Indonesia's Manufacturing Sector during 2020–2024*. https://www.adb.org/publications/policies-manufacturing-sector-indonesia-2020-2024.

ADB and Organisation for Economic Co-operation and Development (OECD). 2015. *Education in Indonesia: Rising to the Challenge*. http://dx.doi.org/10.1787/9789264230750-en.

Allen, E. 2016. Raising Indonesian Labor Productivity. *Nikkei Asian Review*. https://asia.nikkei.com/Economy/Emma-Allen-Raising-Indonesian-labor-productivity.

Andersson, J. et al. 2018. *Is Apparel Manufacturing coming Home? Nearshoring, Automation, and Sustainability – Establishing a Demand-Focused Apparel Value Chain*. McKinsey Apparel, Fashion & Luxury Group. October. https://www.mckinsey.com/~/media/mckinsey/industries/retail/our%20insights/is%20apparel%20manufacturing%20coming%20home/is-apparel-manufacturing-coming-home_vf.ashx.

ASEAN Secretariat. 2018. *ASEAN Key Figures 2018*. https://www.aseanstats.org/wp-content/uploads/2018/12/ASEAN-Key-Figures-2018.pdf.

Arbulu, I. et al. 2018. Industry 4.0: Reinvigorating ASEAN Manufacturing for the Future. *McKinsey & Company*. 8 February. https://www.mckinsey.com/business-functions/operations/our-insights/industry-4-0-reinvigorating-asean-manufacturing-for-the-future.

Asia Philanthropy Circle. 2017. *Catalysing Productive Livelihood: A Guide to Education Interventions with an Accelerated Path to Scale and Impact*. https://www.edumap-indonesia.asiaphilanthropycircle.org/.

Barber, M. 2007. *Instruction to Deliver: Fighting to Transform Britain's Public Services*.

The Behavioural Insights Team, Cabinet Office and Nesta. 2015. Easy, Attractive, Timely, Social: Four Simple Ways to Apply Behavioural Insights. https://www.behaviouralinsights.co.uk/wp-content/uploads/2015/07/BIT-Publication-EAST_FA_WEB.pdf.

Bonoli, G. 2019. Ensuring Economic Security in the Gig Economy. *The Business Times*. https://www.businesstimes.com.sg/opinion/ensuring-economic-security-in-the-gig-economy.

Boston Consulting Group. 2015. *Industry 4.0: The Future of Productivity and Growth in Manufacturing Industries*. https://www.bcg.com/publications/2015/engineered_products_project_business_industry_4_future_productivity_growth_manufacturing_industries.

Chan, S. 2018. Adapting to Industry 4.0 a Top Priority: Ministry. *Khmer Times*. 4 September. https://www.khmertimeskh.com/529898/adapting-to-industry-4-0-a-top-priority-ministry/.

CGS Blog. 2019. *What Industry 4.0 Means for Apparel, Fashion, and Footwear Manufacturers*. 12 February. https://www.cgsinc.com/blog/what-industry-4.0-means-apparel-fashion-and-footwear-manufacturers.

Cornell University, INSEAD, and World Intellectual Property Organization. 2019. *Global Innovation Index 2019: Creating Healthy Lives —The Future of Medical Innovation*. https://www.wipo.int/edocs/pubdocs/en/wipo_pub_gii_2019.pdf.

Chitturu, S. 2017. *Artificial Intelligence and Southeast Asia's Future*. McKinsey Global Institute. September. https://www.mckinsey.com/~/media/McKinsey/Featured%20Insights/Artificial%20Intelligence/AI%20and%20SE%20ASIA%20future/Artificial-intelligence-and-Southeast-Asias-future.ashx.

Daly, E. and S. Singham. 2012. Delivery 2.0: The New Challenge for Governments. *McKinsey & Company*. https://www.mckinsey.com/industries/public-sector/our-insights/delivery-20-the-new-challenge-for-governments.

———. 2020. 10 Actions. https://www.mckinsey.com/about-us/diversity/overview#.

Dang, V. L. and G.T. Yeo. 2018. Weighing the Key Factors to Improve Viet Nam's Logistics System. *The Asian Journal of Shipping and Logistics*. https://www.sciencedirect.com/science/article/pii/S2092521218300774.

Dara, V. 2019. Help Requested for Industry 4.0 Labour. *The Phnom Penh Post*. 17 June. https://www.phnompenhpost.com/national/help-requested-industry-40-labour.

Deloitte. 2015. 3D Opportunity Serves it Up: Additive Manufacturing and Food. https://www2.deloitte.com/us/en/insights/focus/3d-opportunity/3d-printing-in-the-food-industry.html.

Dichter, A. 2018. How to Serve Today's Digital Traveler. *McKinsey & Company*. 19 December. https://www.mckinsey.com/industries/travel-transport-and-logistics/our-insights/how-to-serve-todays-digital-traveler.

Generation Program. 2019. https://www.generation.org/.

Goehrke, S. 2018. Additive Manufacturing Is Driving The Future Of The Automotive Industry. *Forbes*. 5 December. https://www.forbes.com/sites/sarahgoehrke/2018/12/05/additive-manufacturing-is-driving-the-future-of-the-automotive-industry/#2eb708e775cc.

Government of Cambodia. 2015. *Cambodia Industrial Development Policy 2015-2025*. https://www.eurocham-cambodia.org/uploads/97dae-idp_19may15_com_official.pdf.

Government of Cambodia. 2018. *Rectangular Strategy for Growth, Employment, Equity, and Efficiency: Building the Foundation Toward Realizing the Cambodia Vision 2050 Phase IV*. http://cnv.org.kh/wp-content/uploads/2012/10/Rectangular-Strategy-Phase-IV-of-the-Royal-Government-of-Cambodia-of-the-Sixth-Legislature-of-the-National-Assembly-2018-2023.pdf.

Government of Cambodia, Ministry of Commerce. 2019. *Cambodia Trade Integration Strategy 2019–2023*. https://www.moc.gov.kh/Portals/0/Docs/OfficialDocs/CTIS-20190725143301726.pdf.

Government of Cambodia, Ministry of Economy and Finance. 2020. *Cambodia Garment and Textile Strategy*.

Government of Cambodia, National Employment Agency. 2017. *Skills Shortages and Skills Gaps in the Cambodian Labour Market: Evidence from Employer Survey 2017*. http://www.nea.gov.kh/images/survay/ESNS%202017--Final--05282018.pdf.

Government of Cambodia , National Institute of Statistics. 2015. Cambodia Socio Economic Survey 2015. http://www.nis.gov.kh/nis/CSES/Final%20Report%20CSES%202015.pdf.

Government of Indonesia, Ministry of Industry. *Making Indonesia 4.0*. http://www.kemenperin.go.id/kebijakan-industri.

———. *National Industrial Development Master Plan 2015-2035*. https://kemenperin.go.id/ripin.pdf.

———. *National Medium-Term Industrial Development Plan 2015-2019*. http://www.kemenperin.go.id/profil/71/rencana-strategis-kementerian-perindustrian.

Government of Indonesia, Ministry of Manpower. 2019. *Penandatanganan Kerja Sama "BLK" Komunitas Tahap I Tahun 2019 antara Kementerian Ketenagakerjaan dengan Lembaga Penerima Bantuan*. 20 February. https://www.kemenkumham.go.id/publikasi/siaran-pers/penandatanganan-kerja-sama-"BLK"-komunitas-tahap-i-tahun-2019-antara-kementerian-ketenagakerjaan-dengan-lembaga-penerima-bantuan.

Government of Indonesia, Ministry of Research, Technology and Higher Education. Policies and Programs. https://international.ristekdikti.go.id/policies-and-programs/.

Government of Indonesia, Sekretariat Kabinet Republik Indonesia. 2016. Presidential Decree No. 9 Year 2016 on Revitalizing SMKs to Improve the Quality and Competitiveness of Indonesian Human Resources. https://kemdikbud.go.id/main/files/download/e451d9ec3a04121.

Government of Malaysia, Department of Skills Development. Malaysian Skill Certificate (SKM). https://www.dsd.gov.my/index.php/en/service/malaysian-skills-certificate.

Government of Malaysia, Ministry of Higher Education and Malaysian Qualifications Agency 2011. *Malaysian Qualifications Framework*. http://www2.mqa.gov.my.

Government of the Philippines, Department of Budget and Management. 2019. *TESDA Budget nearly Doubles in 2019*. https://www.dbm.gov.ph/index.php/secretary-s-corner/press-releases/list-of-press-releases/1247-tesda-budget-nearly-doubles-in-2019.

Government of the Philippines, Technical Education and Skills Development Authority. National Technical Skills Development Plan. http://www.tesda.gov.ph/About/TESDA/47.

Government of Singapore, Ministry of Education. 2016. *Formation of the Council for Skills, Innovation and Productivity* (Press Release). https://www.moe.gov.sg/news/press-releases/formation-of-the-council-for-skills--innovation-and-productivity.

Government of Singapore, Ministry of Trade and Industry. 2017. Media factsheet- Industry Transformation Maps. https://www.mti.gov.sg/-/media/MTI/ITM/General/Fact-sheet-on-Industry-Transformation-Maps---revised-as-of-31-Mar-17.pdf.

Gül, K. and M. Gül. 2018. The Effect of the Fourth Industrial Revolution on Tourism. *Balikesir University* (Working Paper Series) https://www.researchgate.net/publication/330909577_THE_EFFECT_OF_FOURTH_INDUSTRIAL_REVOLUTION_ON_TOURISM.

Hasnan, L. 2019. Philippines's Fast-Growing Gig Economy. *The ASEAN Post*. 9 October. https://theaseanpost.com/article/philippines-fast-growing-gig-economy.

IBPAP. 2014. Talent Deep Dive: An Analysis of Talent Availability for the Information Technology and Business Process Management Industry in 10 Provinces in the Philippines.

International Labour Organization (ILO). 2015. *Rural Development and Employment Opportunities in Cambodia; How Can a National Employment Policy Contribute Toward Realization of Decent Work in Rural Areas?* https://www.ilo.org/wcmsp5/groups/public/---asia/---ro-bangkok/documents/publication/wcms_228280.pdf.

ILO. 2018. *Improving Practical Skills of Job Seekers through Apprenticeship*. https://www.ilo.org/jakarta/info/public/pr/WCMS_636126/lang--en/index.htm.

Indonesia Investments. 2018. Widodo Launches Road Map for Industry 4.0: Making Indonesia 4.0. https://www.indonesia-investments.com/business/business-columns/widodo-launches-road map-for-industry-4.0-making-indonesia-4.0/item8711.

International Federation of Robotics. 2019. Why Robot Sales in China will Survive Slowdown in Car Production. https://ifr.org/post/Why-robot-sales-in-China-will-survive-slowdown-in-car-production.

Istance, D. and A. Paniagua. 2019. *Learning to Leapfrog: Innovative Pedagogies to Transform Education.* Center for Universal Education at Brookings Institution. https://www.brookings.edu/wp-content/uploads/2019/09/Learning-to-Leapfrog-InnovativePedagogiestoTransformEducation-Web.pdf.

Iswara, M. A. and M. I. Gorbiano . 2019. Jokowi's Preemployment Card Program under Scrutiny. *The Jakarta Post.* 12 August. https://www.thejakartapost.com/news/2019/08/12/jokowi-s-preemployment-card-program-under-scrutiny.html.

The Jakarta Post. 2016. Five Plans to Upskill Indonesia's Workforce. 4 May. https://www.thejakartapost.com/adv/2016/05/04/five-plans-to-upskill-indonesias-workforce.html.

KellyOCG. 2018. From Workforce to Workfit. https://www.kellyocg.com/insights/featured-content/whitepapers/from-workforce-to-workfit/.

Ketelhut, D. et al. 2009. A Multi-User Virtual Environment for Building and Assessing Higher Order Inquiry Skills in Science. *British Journal of Educational Technology.* https://onlinelibrary.wiley.com/doi/abs/10.1111/j.1467-8535.2009.01036.x.

Koemsoeun, S. 2020. Ministry Changes its Name, Scope of Operations. *The Phnom Penh Post.* 26 January: https://phnompenhpost.com/national/ministry-changes-its-name-scope-operations.

Kong, M. 2019. *Long-term Policy Framework for Cambodia's Digital Economy.* (Presentation) https://set.odi.org/wp-content/uploads/2019/11/Presentation-on-Concept-Note-of-DE.pdf.

Lewandowski, P. et al. 2019. Technology, Skills and Globalization: Explaining International Differences in Routine and Nonroutine Work using Survey Data. *IBS working paper.* April.

Lee, J. W. 2016. How Can Asia Close its Emerging Skills Gap? *World Economic Forum Regional Agenda.* https://www.weforum.org/agenda/2016/01/how-can-asia-close-its-emerging-skills-gap.

Maclean, R, S., Jagannathan, and J. Sarvi, eds. 2012. *Skills Development for Inclusive and Sustainable Growth in Developing Asia-Pacific.* https://www.adb.org/publications/skills-development-inclusive-and-sustainable-growth-developing-asia-pacific.

Masters, K. 2017. The Impact of Industry 4.0 on the Automotive Industry. https://blog.flexis.com/the-impact-of-industry-4.0-on-the-automotive-industry.

Mekong Strategy Partners and Raintree Development. 2018. Cambodia's Vibrant Startup Ecosystem. https://static1.squarespace.com/static/56a87acd05f8e263f7b16c7f/t/5c9b0762085229887ba9af72/1553663849501/Cambodian_Tech_Startup_Report_Final_250319.pdf.

Microsoft. 2018. *Closing the STEM Gap: Why Stem Classes and Careers Still Lack Girls and What We Can Do About It.* https://query.prod.cms.rt.microsoft.com/cms/api/am/binary/RE1UMWz.

Microsoft. 2018. *The Future Computed*. https://blogs.microsoft.com/wp-content/uploads/2018/02/The-Future-Computed_2.8.18.pdf.

Microsoft and AlphaBeta. 2019. *Preparing For AI: The Implications of Artificial Intelligence for Jobs and Skills In Asian Economies*. https://news.microsoft.com/apac/2019/08/26/preparing-for-ai-the-implications-of-artificial-intelligence-for-jobs-and-skills-in-asian-economies/.

Microsoft and International Data Corporation (IDC). 2018. Microsoft – IDC Study: Artificial Intelligence to Nearly Double the Rate of Innovation in Asia Pacific by 2021. https://news.microsoft.com/apac/2019/02/20/microsoft-idc-study-artificial-intelligence-to-nearly-double-the-rate-of-innovation-in-asia-pacific-by-2021/.

Ng, J. S. 2018. Focus on Skills, Not Paper Qualifications, to Embrace Technological Change: Lawrence Wong. *Straits Times*. 5 May. https://www.straitstimes.com/world/lawrence-wong-focus-on-skills-not-paper-qualifications-to-embrace-technological-change.

Organisation for Economic Co-operation and Development (OECD). 2010. *Learning for Jobs - The OECD International Survey of VET Systems: First Results and Technical Report*. https://www.oecd.org/education/skills-beyond-school/47334855.pdf.

OECD. 2012. *Skills Development Pathways in Asia*. https://www.oecd.org/cfe/leed/Skills%20Development%20Pathways%20in%20Asia_FINAL%20VERSION.pdf.

———. 2018. *The Future of Social Protection: What Works for Non-Standard Workers?* https://doi.org/10.1787/9789264306943-en.

onebillion. onecourse: one app that delivers reading, writing and numeracy. https://onebillion.org/onecourse/app/. https://onebillion.org/onecourse/app/.

Orbeta, A. et al. 2016. Are Higher Education Institutions Responsive to Changes in the Labor Market? *Philippine Institute for Development Studies* (Discussion Paper Series). https://dirp4.pids.gov.ph/websitecms/CDN/PUBLICATIONS/pidsdps1608.pdf.

Oxford Economics. 2018. *Technology and the Future of ASEAN Jobs: The Impact of AI on Workers in ASEAN's Six Largest Economies*. https://www.oxfordeconomics.com/recent-releases/dd577680-7297-4677-aa8f-450da197e132.

Oxford Internet Institute. 2019. Online Labour Index. https://ilabour.oii.ox.ac.uk/online-labour-index/.

Pathways for Prosperity Commission. 2019. *Positive Disruption: Health and Education in the Digital Age*. https://pathwayscommission.bsg.ox.ac.uk/positive-disruption.

Payoneer. The Global Gig Economy Index: Q2 2019. https://explore.payoneer.com/q2_global_freelancing_index/.

PayPal. 2018. PayPal Releases Global Freelancer Insights. *PayPal Stories*. https://www.paypal.com/stories/us/paypal-releases-global-freelancer-insights.

Prospera and AlphaBeta Advisors. 2019. *Capturing Indonesia's Automation Potential.* https://www.alphabeta.com/wp-content/uploads/2019/08/capturing-indonesias-automation-potential.pdf.

RAND. Indonesian Family Life Survey (IFLS). https://www.rand.org/well-being/social-and-behavioral-policy/data/FLS/IFLS.html.

Revfine. 2018. *4 Ways Facial Recognition Can Be Used in the Travel Industry.* https://www.revfine.com/facial-recognition-travel-industry/.

———. 2018. *How Artificial Intelligence is Changing the Travel Industry.* https://www.revfine.com/artificial-intelligence-travel-industry/.

———. 2018. *How Blockchain Technology is Transforming the Travel Industry.* https://www.revfine.com/blockchain-technology-travel-industry/.

———. 2018. *How the Internet of Things (IoT) can Benefit the Travel Industry.* https://www.revfine.com/internet-of-things-travel-industry/.

Rodrigo, P. 2017. Half of All Indonesian Employees "May be Underqualified," *CIPD.* 10 May. https://www.cipd.asia/news/hr-news/half-indonesians-under-qualified.

Schwab, K. 2017. *The Fourth Industrial Revolution.* https://books.google.com.sg/books?hl=en&lr=&id=ST_FDAAAQBAJ&oi=fnd&pg=PR7&dq=klaus+schwab+fourth+industrial+revolution&ots=DTnvbTqvTQ&sig=aOLqcUCFsLKbNpjWa5kr2Sjzhu4#v=onepage&q=klaus%20schwab%20fourth%20industrial%20revolution&f=false.

SITA. *Air Transport IT Insights 2018.* https://www.sita.aero/resources/type/surveys-reports/air-transport-it-insights-2018.

SkillsFuture Singapore. 2019. Funding Support for Employers. https://www.ssg.gov.sg/programmes-and-initiatives/funding/funding-for-employer-based-training.html.

SkillsFuture Singapore. 2019. Skills Framework. https://www.skillsfuture.sg/skills-framework.

SME Corp Malaysia. Skills Upgrading Programme. https://www.smecorp.gov.my/index.php/en/slides/86-program-sme/103/skills-upgrading-programme (accessed August 2019).

Spector, J. M. and S. Ma. 2019. Inquiry and Critical Thinking Skills for the Next Generation: From Artificial Intelligence Back to Human Intelligence. *Smart Learning Environments.* 11 September. https://slejournal.springeropen.com/articles/10.1186/s40561-019-0088-z.

Spiess, R. 2019. Ready for a (Digital) Revolution? *Southeast Asia Global.* 28 March. https://southeastasiaglobe.com/cambodia-ready-for-a-digital-revolution/.

Sullivan, R. 2019. Increased Role of Robots in Food Manufacturing. *Food Quality & Safety.* 25 February. https://www.foodqualityandsafety.com/article/increased-role-of-robots-in-food-manufacturing/.

Tang, S. K. 2019. Singapore Businesses Not Investing Enough in Employee Training: SBF Survey. *Channel News Asia*. https://www.channelnewsasia.com/news/business/singapore-companies-not-investing-employee-training-sbf-survey-11134230.

Telecommunications Regulator of Cambodia. 2015. *Cambodian ICT Masterplan 2020*. https://www.trc. gov.kh/summary-on-cambodian-ict-masterplan-2020/.

TrekkSoft. 2019. *Travel Trends Report 2019*. https://www.trekksoft.com/en/resources/ebooks/travel-trends-report-2019 .

Triyono, M. B. and D. E. Murniati. 2018. Alignment of the Curriculum to the Development of the Industrial World (Revitalization Program of Vocational High Schools in Indonesia. *TVET-Online*. https://www.voced.edu.au/content/ngv%3A80395.

United Nations Educational, Scientific, and Cultural Organization (UNESCO). 2017. *Towards Quality Assurance of Technical and Vocational Education and Training*. https://unesdoc.unesco.org/ark:/48223/pf0000259282.

UNESDOC Digital Library. 2017. *Lifelong Learning in Transformation: Promising Practices in Southeast Asia*. https://unesdoc.unesco.org/ark:/48223/pf0000253603.

UNESCO Institute for Lifelong Learning. *Japan: Basic Plan for the Promotion of Education, issued in 2008*. http://uil.unesco.org/document/japan-basic-plan-promotion-education-issued-2008.

———. *Republic of Korea: The 3rd National Lifelong Learning Promotion Plan: 2017, issued in 2013*. http://uil.unesco.org/document/republic-korea-3rd-national-lifelong-learning-promotion-plan-2017-issued-2013.

———. *Vietnam: Framework on Building a learning society in the period 2012-2020, issued in 2013*. http://uil.unesco.org/document/vietnam-framework-building-learning-society-period-2012-2020-issued-2013 .

USAID & FHI. 2015. Workforce Connections – Analysis of Skills Demand in Indonesia.

VAR Insights. 2010. YCH Group Selects Intermec Fixed Vehicle Computer to Improve Supply Chain Management. https://www.varinsights.com/doc/ych-group-selects-intermec-fixed-vehicle-0003.

Woetzl, J. et al. 2014. *Southeast Asia at the Crossroads: Three Paths to Prosperity*. McKinsey Global Institute. November. https://www.mckinsey.com/~/media/McKinsey/Featured%20Insights/Asia%20Pacific/Three%20paths%20to%20sustained%20economic%20growth%20in%20Southeast%20Asia/MGI%20SE%20Asia_Executive%20summary_November%202014.ashx.

World Bank and AT Kearney. 2018. *Readiness for the Future of Production Report 2018*. http://www3.weforum.org/docs/FOP_Readiness_Report_2018.pdf.

World Economic Forum (WEF). 2018. *The Future of Jobs Report 2018*. http://www3.weforum.org/docs/WEF_Future_of_Jobs_2018.pdf.

WEF. 2019. *Towards a Reskilling Revolution: Industry-Led Action for the Future of Work.* http://www3. weforum.org/docs/WEF_Towards_a_Reskilling_Revolution.pdf.

Yasih, D. W. P. and A. R. Alamsyah. 2018. Can Grab and GoJek Drivers in Indonesia Build a Solid Union? *The Conversation.* 18 April. https://theconversation.com/can-grab-and-gojek-drivers-in-indonesia-build-a-solid-union-95032.

www.ingramcontent.com/pod-product-compliance
Lightning Source LLC
Chambersburg PA
CBHW050048220326

41599CB00045B/7325